How to Listen, Hear, and Validate:

Break Through Invisible Barriers and Transform Your Relationships

By Patrick King
Social Interaction and
Conversation Coach at
www.PatrickKingConsulting.com

Table of Contents

Chapter 1. Validation As a Communication Skill

Picture a couple having a discussion one day, that quickly turns heated. It goes a little something like this:

A: "So the doctor called and they have the results from my test back..."

B: "Oh my god, so what was the result?"

A: "Well, they said everything's clear. The first test was just a fluke, apparently. There's nothing to worry about."

B: "What?! That's amazing! I'm so glad to hear that! You must be so relieved..."

A: "Well, actually, I don't know..."

B: "You're not relieved?"

A: "It's hard to explain. I guess I'm a bit...disappointed? That sounds strange. But I was really kind of expecting a scary result. And I almost feel a bit let down? I know that sounds silly..."

B: "That is silly. You're crazy. You have no idea how lucky you are. We should go out to celebrate."

A: "Uh, can we not? I'm just not feeling it..."

B: "What's wrong with you? You're being ridiculous. You don't mean to say you wish the test was positive? That's crazy..."

And so on. Can you imagine A continuing to try and explain how they really felt, with B rejecting the whole idea as bizarre, or even getting a little angry and judging A for not being grateful or excited? Consider how the conversation could have gone otherwise:

A: "So the doctor called and they have the results from my test back..."

B: "Oh my god, so what was the result?"

A: *"Well, they said everything's clear. The first test was just a fluke, apparently. There's nothing to worry about."*

B: *"What?! That's amazing! I'm so glad to hear that! You must be so relieved..."*

A: *"Well, actually, I don't know..."*

B: *"You're not relieved?"*

A: *"It's hard to explain. I guess I'm a bit...disappointed? That sounds strange. But I was really kind of expecting a scary result. And I almost feel a bit let down? I know that sounds silly..."*

B: *"No, it's not silly. Can you explain what you mean? I'm pretty relieved to hear you're OK, but you seem a little unsure..."*

A: *"Yeah, I don't know...maybe I had already mentally prepared myself for it being positive..."*

B: *"Tell me more."*

Imagine the conversation then moving on to A explaining how they feel and why, with B listening closely, not so they could argue against A's feelings, but so they could better understand and support them, even if they did seem strange.

What's the difference in the second conversation? The answer is validation.

In this book, we're going to be looking at the power of validation: what it is, what it isn't, and how it can be used to deepen relationships, grow empathy and improve communication.

Validation is something that seems easy to understand conceptually, but can be subtle and difficult to grasp in real life. In trying to understand what validation is, it can be helpful to look at what it *isn't*.

In the first conversation, B's attitude was dismissive. By calling A silly, crazy, and ridiculous, the message was clear: the way that A felt (and by extension, A themselves) was wrong. In fact, B asks, "What's wrong with you?" and then proceeds to say how A *should* feel. Granted, this is an extreme example (B is definitely a jerk in this scenario!), but we can clearly see the spirit of invalidation.

When we invalidate someone, we deny their experience. We contradict them, undermine them, doubt them, disagree with them or judge them. We tell them that what they feel or perceive is wrong, mistaken, useless, undesirable. We tell them that what they are going through is not really justifiable, legitimate or "logical." Sometimes, we may act as though the way they feel is in violation of some objective reality, and they should be ashamed of their feelings. To sum it up, invalidation is about **not accepting** the person in front of us, as they are.

When we invalidate someone, what we might be responding to is their emotional reality, their thoughts, speech, behavior, beliefs, perspectives or ideas—but in the process we may more or less invalidate them as individuals. There's a fine line between saying "your reaction is too much" and saying "*you* are too much."

It may seem like invalidation is quite an aggressive thing to do, but in reality, invalidations can be small, subtle, and even take place under the guise of genuine concern or an attempt to help. For example, many parents will tell a frightened child not to be so silly, and that there's nothing to be scared about. Though they intend to help, the message the child hears is "you're wrong somehow." If they *shouldn't* be scared, but they *are*, what does that say about them?

Likewise, consider these small, yet nevertheless invalidating statements:

"You like mayonnaise with your fries? Weird."

"Hey, don't take it so personally!"

"You're upset about your stressful job? What about people who don't even *have* jobs—how do you think that makes them feel?"

"You're not being reasonable right now, calm down."

"Lots of people say they don't want kids—but you'll change your mind, just wait!"

Though we've all been the recipients of statements like the ones above—or maybe said things like this to others—it's difficult to pinpoint just how invalidating they can be. What's missing in the above sentiments? What makes them feel so bad to hear?

In the chapters that follow, we'll understand **validation as the act of acknowledging and accepting another person's experience, i.e. communicating that it is inherently valid.** Validation doesn't mean we agree with the other person, or like what they are experiencing, or even understand it. But it does mean we recognize that their experience has the right to exist as it is. If we see someone is angry, we could try to push back against the anger, argue with it, deny it or avoid it; or, we could acknowledge that the person *is* angry, and that's the way it is.

Many people struggle with giving validation because they genuinely cannot see the point. If someone is having a different internal experience to them, or their perceptions don't match with what they consider "objective reality," they seem to forget about the need to be compassionate, understanding or kind.

Imagine, for example, that Jeremy has started to hear voices that aren't there, and he's petrified. He talks to a close friend about his concerns, but the friend immediately tells him that the voices aren't there, he *knows* they aren't there, so what's the problem? The friend may start to talk about medications to get the voices to go away, but in his own way, he tells Jeremy that being afraid of imaginary voices doesn't actually make sense.

Now imagine that Jeremy goes to a different friend. He shares his concerns and this friend looks not at what's real and not real, what's a reasonable reaction and what isn't, but how Jeremy is actually feeling. They tell him that being afraid is normal and understandable. In other words, the objective facts of his experience are not as important as his internal, subjective experience. The first friend invalidated this experience, whereas the second validated it.

People who are quite practically minded may have trouble with the concept of validation because it seems more natural for them to look for obvious solutions, to gather data, to identify problems in the "real world" and fix them. They may mistakenly think that validation means agreeing with something that's wrong, or doing nothing to actually remedy the problem.

But validation is an important and necessary part of human communication, even if it is not focused on verifying or solving an issue.

When we focus only on "facts," we may miss the emotional content—which is often one of the more important reasons for communicating in the first place. Most of us like to think we are empathic and understanding, but mastering real validation can take some practice, and we all miss the mark sometimes. After all, who hasn't tried to "cheer up" a friend when they felt down, reassuring them that things weren't really so bad?

Why validation is so important

All human beings want to feel that they are, at their core, acceptable, even lovable.

We all want to feel that other people see us, acknowledge who we are, and generally find us to have value. When you practice the art of validation, you learn how to give this experience to others. When we validate people, we accept them for who they really are. What better way to be a good friend, partner or parent?

When you validate someone, you give them real support, letting them know that they are not alone. Life can be confusing and difficult for all of us, but when we are genuinely validated, we can feel reassured that we are on the right path, and that our experience is normal.

Willpower is great, but any single person only has so much of it. Haven't you felt stronger and more capable when you had the support of many other people behind you? Picture someone who is working really hard to overcome a food addiction and lose weight. They may feel completely defeated and alone when, months later, nobody has even noticed their progress. On the other hand, having work colleagues check in regularly, acknowledge the hard journey they're on, and even recognize the results can make it so much easier to carry on.

In today's world, people are arguably more isolated and divided than ever before, with many having little to draw on in terms of family or community. But if we don't have fellow human beings to accompany us through life's challenges, to acknowledge our presence and even enjoy it, to reflect back to us who we are and the effect of our actions—well, we can soon start to feel like we don't really exist at all. You can probably remember a time when someone paid you a really thoughtful compliment about who you were as a person, and how great it made you feel. Compare that to the crushing sense of alienation you have when a person you thought knew you well buys you a completely bizarre gift that you hate!

Of course, it's not just about how many people are in your life; without real validation and acceptance, it's possible to feel completely alone and unseen in a room full of people. We may feel lost or out of place, even in our own families, or like foreigners even in our own countries. An absence of genuine validation is behind someone who, after twenty years of marriage, can look at their spouse and say, "I have no idea who you even are."

Being seen and heard, on the other hand, gives life a solidity and a sense of meaning. It adds richness, color and depth to our days. When others witness and confirm our experience, it's as though it becomes more real and manageable for us. If you can learn to really see and validate people as they are, you are simultaneously giving them and yourself a wonderful gift that's in pretty short supply in today's world. When we are validated, we feel more resilient to life's problems, and can regulate our emotions more effectively.

We feel like *ourselves*; when others see and acknowledge us, it is as confirming to our identity as looking into a mirror and seeing an image look back at us. Through others' sincere response, we learn about who we are. We see them react to us, care for us, listen to us, and in so doing it seems like our persona takes shape, and we can see the outlines of ourselves more clearly.

It goes a little deeper, too. When we validate someone, we not only see the person in front of us, but *accept* them, completely. We communicate, with our nonjudgmental attention, that they are worth knowing, and they are important. Even if we don't fully comprehend what it's like to be in another person's shoes, it's still wonderful to show that we care enough to *try* and comprehend it. Many parents, for example, cannot really get inside their teenage children's heads, but sometimes all that's needed is for that teenager to feel that their mom or dad cares enough to make the effort in the first place.

This isn't to say that validation is only beneficial for the person receiving it. When validation flows from one person to another, both benefit. The shared relationship instantly becomes more authentic, more trusting and more honest. When people feel seen and accepted, they are more able to return the kindness to others, strengthening those connections. In fact, there may now be evidence that being validated by someone can literally cause changes in the neurotransmitters released in your brain.

Validation is about affirming someone else's emotional reality, but it's also about recognizing that they live in a completely different world to you, and inhabit a perspective entirely separate from your own. If you can undertake any conversation with the spirit of validation, you are able to respect and honor the fact that the other person is not you, and doesn't think like you. Validation encourages deeper understanding. Not only will this make you a better communicator, but it will expand your world view, and you may even learn something in the process.

Isn't validation the same as empathy?

In reading about the virtues and benefits of practicing validation, you might have wondered whether it's the same thing as simply being kind and compassionate. In many ways, these concepts do overlap to some degree. A person with good validation skills may on the surface be indistinguishable from someone who is empathetic, nonjudgmental, or simply skilled at showing interest in others. But there are differences.

Showing **sympathy** is acknowledging someone else's experience, but as seen through our own frame of reference. For example, knowing that someone else is nervous giving a speech because you yourself would be anxious doing the same thing.

Showing **empathy** is looking inside someone else's experiences and feeling what that feels like, from that person's point of view, and not your own. For example, you can imagine what it feels like to be the person terrified of giving a speech even though you yourself love public speaking.

Showing **validation**, however, is a little different. This is where we communicate that we have seen or heard the other person's experience, and that it has *inherent validity*. So, we can listen to our friend telling us how scared they are to give their speech and acknowledge it, and take that at face value. Our own feelings on public speaking don't matter at all, and in fact, nobody else's opinion matters either.

When we acknowledge the inherent validity of someone else's experience, we are doing something a little different from having empathy. When we are sympathetic or empathetic, we are shifting or expanding frames of reference to better understand another person's experience. But with validation, we take their experience as the only frame of reference that matters. Someone's feelings or thoughts might not be pleasant, or sensical, or popular, or permissible, or even understandable. But they are nevertheless valid, because they are there, and they exist.

As you can see, it's a subtle point that can make rather a large difference when put into practice. Empathy can often lead people to feel validated, but not necessarily. For example, someone might feel very sorry for a friend who is having difficulties, and empathize completely, while still believing that their experience is not completely valid—i.e. "I genuinely feel bad for you, but

I still think you're just overreacting." We'll explore how to combine empathy *and* validation later on in the book.

Validation—one of the clearest ways to express care

There's the stereotypical argument that is said to occasionally unfold between men and women: the woman may be upset about something, and tells the man about it, who then proceeds to try and find ways to fix the problem, despite the woman claiming over and over, "I just want you to listen!"

Validation has a big role to play in validating negative feelings or supporting those experiencing stress. Psychologists originally explored its power in helping people who feel suicidal or deeply distressed, but soon put the principle of validation at the center of all their work. After all, when people seek mental health care, they are often simply seeking comfort and reassurance.

Researchers Tian, Solomon and Brisini at Penn State University published a 2020 paper in the *Journal of Communication* describing how validation can be used to improve our normal ways of comforting people. They found that the language people use can have a massive impact.

For example, most people don't respond well to being told (subtly or not so subtly) how to feel. For example, most of us bristle at platitudes like "there there, don't cry now" or "come on, try to look at the good side." Instead, it may be more effective to simply enquire about how the person actually is feeling, rather than telling them to feel some other way. This way, they can express themselves and reach their own conclusions, deciding for themselves what action to take next.

The authors also found that it's best to avoid language that minimizes feelings. For example, if someone has just confided in you that they are feeling severely depressed, it's obviously not a good idea to shake it off as "the blues" and tell them they just need a good night's sleep. It's true that these comments may come from a good place, but they could actually have the opposite effect. If someone feels judged, controlled, ignored or ridiculed, they'll obviously feel less inclined to take the help offered, even if it's sincere.

The trouble is that these sorts of comments may well have been beneficial in another context. Offering advice or helpful suggestions is usually just people's way of trying to be useful. They may indeed be very skilled communicators and have the best of intentions. But, importantly, **validation is not like other communication techniques**. The purpose and outcome of validation is completely different to, say, offering advice or giving helpful feedback.

To return to the stereotypical argument we began with, the man might say (quite rightly) that he is attempting to help, that his solution would work, and that the woman is being ridiculous by continuing to be upset when a perfectly good solution is right in front of her. But the woman might say (quite rightly) that she hasn't asked for advice or problem-solving; she wants comfort, that is, validation.

In a way, validation digs a little deeper than most communication skills and techniques, and gets to the heart of our emotional experience. You can be an excellent listener, compassionate, intelligent and great at offering useful advice, but none of it matters if what is needed is direct validation.

So, we've seen the kind of things we shouldn't say, but what *do* you say to someone to validate their experience?

Remember, when we provide validation, we are communicating that someone's experience, and they themselves, are inherently valid. So, we can use phrases like:

- "It's understandable you'd feel that way."

- "Yes, that makes sense. I can see why you say that."

- "It's perfectly normal that you think that."

- "I'm sorry that you're having a hard time with this."

- "Can you tell me more about how you're feeling?"

- "I can see why you feel XYZ."

When validating someone, sometimes the best thing we can do for them is to simply create a little space for them to be as they are. Often, we're compelled to jump in and say something, *anything*, but that's just because we ourselves are uncomfortable. It's possible to communicate a great deal of compassion and acceptance with simple sounds like "uh-huh" and "mmm" or simply listening and nodding. This way, you are lavishing your full attention of the other person, without trying to push your own interpretation.

Validation rests on **centering the other person**. This means that the person and their experience are the priority—and other people's opinions, society's expectations, judgments, and criticisms are set aside. To center someone means to acknowledge that the individual themselves is the ultimate authority on their own inner experience. So, if they express that they are feeling scared even though it looks to you and everyone else like anger, you take their word for it and assume that yes, in their internal experience, they *are* scared.

Validating the right way and in the right moment

Is validation always the right approach? Are there some things we shouldn't validate?

For example, should you really validate someone's experience if they are talking about or planning harm to themselves or others? On a less serious note, should you validate someone's complaint—when it's the fiftieth complaint you've already heard from them that day? Do you have to validate someone's experience when, to be frank, you're exhausted and you'd rather they didn't dump it all on you?

Validation can indeed have unintended consequences, and isn't a cure-all. There are times when this strategy is less appropriate, and may even have negative outcomes. Validation is undoubtedly one of the best relationship and communication tools, but it shouldn't be used with everyone, in every event. We still need to carefully evaluate the situation, observe the consequences of our actions and adapt accordingly.

Though we don't have the scope to explore the topic of narcissism or personality disorders fully in this book, it's worth mentioning that we should proceed with caution when a person has a seemingly bottomless need for validation. Narcissists lack self-awareness or the ability to empathize, and will typically be unable to connect meaningfully with you, no matter how much or how genuinely you validate them. They might soak up validation and demand more and more, trampling your boundaries in the process. You might quickly find yourself embroiled in an unhealthy or codependent dynamic.

Does this mean you should never validate a narcissist's experience? Of course not. It just means you need to be a little more careful with how you do so, while respecting your own needs and boundaries. Since all human beings need and deserve validation, there's nobody who should be denied it—but whether *you* should be the person to give it in any one moment is for you to decide.

Validation is almost always a good thing, with the caveat that it is sometimes *not enough on its own*. With this in mind, there are a few red flags to watch out for:

Red flag 1: Aggressive, illegal or inappropriate acts

Perhaps someone confesses to you something bad they've done, or plan to do. Perhaps someone is being threatening and unreasonable. There's no reason why you cannot listen, validate their experience, and ask questions. There's no reason not to have compassion. However, validation on its own is dangerously close to being complicit. Use understanding and compassion, but try to get the other person to take beneficial action, or, in extreme cases, alert authorities yourself.

Red flag 2: Energy vampires

We all feel vulnerable sometimes, and need validation and support. But if you're dealing with someone who wants to sap the life out of you *constantly* while never taking any concrete steps to help themselves, you may need to tighten up your boundaries. Validation is great, but you may actually help them more by saying, "That sounds tough. What are you going to do about it?"

Red flag 3: Someone seeking advice or clarity

Validation always feels good. But sometimes, what really puts a person's mind at ease is knowledge and understanding. If someone is anxious about a performance review at work, for example, it might be more appropriate to stay professional and address their actual concerns with facts and grounded reassurance, rather than focusing on their emotional reality. Depending on the person or the situation, being told "I'm so sorry you're worried about your performance review" doesn't feel as good as being told "you're performing in the upper third of your class, don't worry, you're fine."

In truth, there's very little harm to be done when all you're doing is listening and accepting the person in front of you. Nevertheless, it's worth asking "is this helping?" periodically and adapting according to your honest answer.

Takeaways

- When we validate someone, we convey our acceptance of that person's experiences, emotions, thoughts, and realities. Conversely, when we invalidate someone, we deny or minimize the importance of their issues and needs. Though validation is a common word these days, it's not always clear how best to or even why we should engage in it. The fact is that every person's experience is inherently valid and instead of exercising judgement, we should try and accept people as they are. However, acceptance must not be confused with agreement.

- The concept of validation is especially relevant in our present age because of how socially isolated we are as individuals. Validating someone is a way of expressing solidarity with them, and makes the other person feel heard and understood. It adds a richness and sense of ease to life that would otherwise be missing if we felt that we have to go through life's travails alone and without anyone else's support.

- Many people tend to confuse sympathy, empathy, and validation, and there is indeed significant overlap between the three concepts. However, sympathy is when we see other's experiences through our own lens and react accordingly. When empathizing, we try to relate to other's experiences the way they are experiencing them. Lastly, validation is merely expressing your belief that someone else's experience is inherently valid.

- It's natural to wonder to what extent and how often we should validate others. We can't always validate things, especially when doing so could have adverse effects. For example, validating someone's aggressive and potentially dangerous behavior is a bad idea. Similarly, we must be wary of energy vampire who suck the life out of you by endlessly complaining without taking any concrete steps to ameliorate their situation. Lastly, giving unsolicited advice is generally unadvisable, but if someone is actively looking for guidance from you, substituting it with validation isn't a good idea because it isn't serving any purpose.

Chapter 2. Validation — The Basic Steps

In this chapter, we'll be taking a closer look at *what to actually do and say* when validating someone. We've considered a few key phrases, but validation can occur on several different levels, not all of them applicable in every context. Deciding when and how to offer validation is a skill in itself; in this chapter, we'll look at some frameworks to help us organize our approach.

Validation as Communicating Acceptance

Psychologist Marsha Linehan proposes an interesting and useful framework we can use to help us better understand the process of validation. As we saw in the previous section, validation isn't always appropriate or helpful, but this is often a question of degree—how far to go and what *kind* of validation to give.

According to Linehan, there are six progressive levels of validation, each one building on the one before it. This means if you want to offer level 5 validation, you need to have gone through levels 1 to 4 first. However, you don't have to reach level 5—some situations will call only for some levels, without proceeding further. In certain situations, it might not be necessary or even possible to go beyond a certain level.

In any case, with this model we can see validation as a kind of *communicated acceptance.* Remember, acceptance is not agreement or approval (or even understanding!), but it is prioritizing emotional connection even when there is conflict or difference of opinion.

Level 1 is **being present** with the other person. For example, being still with them, listening closely, paying attention, nodding your head, making eye contact, or letting them know you're there by placing a hand on their shoulder. The best way to be present with someone is to engage in "active listening." You must give the other person non-verbal signals like those that have been mentioned, as well as verbal signals like a "yes" or "go on" intermittently. This acts as feedback for the other person and they automatically become more open and honest with you as a result. Being distracted by your phone while someone pours their heart out to you is obviously not being present, but then again, launching into insensitive "advice" and immediately sharing your opinion also removes your attention and presence from the moment.

In level 1, the biggest hurdle can be acceptance of *ourselves and our emotions* without judgment, so we can resist escaping into denial or justifications just to fill the silence. Some of us can be uncomfortable with intense emotions because they force us to confront our own experiences with situations similar to those the other person is facing. Even someone expressing happiness can be disconcerting to us if we're going through a rough patch. Try not to make your own reaction the focus. Try not to steer away from the emotion being expressed. This will inspire trust and comfort in the other person.

Level 2 is practicing **accurate reflection**. This is when we offer a genuine response that summarizes what we've heard and seen. A lot of people struggle with this step because they simply don't think they have anything valuable to offer, and it adds to the discomfort one might experience in step 1 as well. If this sounds like you, remember that you only have to show the person that you listened to them when they were talking; you need not provide any original input or insight that they missed. It can be as simple as saying, "It sounds like you're having a hard time right now."

The challenge here is to reflect without sounding patronizing, insincere or judgmental. Tone of voice is everything! This is especially true if you're disagreeing with the person in this step. Remember, validation does not always mean agreement. If your friend is narrating an incident about how he feels he isn't working as hard as other employees, you don't have to say that it's okay to feel that way or somehow justify his not working as hard. You can simply say, "Maybe you're being too hard on yourself." What matters is the authenticity of your reflection, not whether it reinforces what the other person is saying. Maybe you disagreeing will make them see that they were indeed being too hard on themselves for some reason.

Level 3 is, for want of a better word, **mindreading**, i.e. trying to guess the other person's thoughts and feelings. Obviously, this can be tricky, and we all differ in our "emotional literacy" and ability to read others. On top of that, people are not always sure what they themselves feel, and may be used to expressing one thing while feeling another, or masking their true experience completely. This step is about trying to put names on possible emotions and thoughts. As you can see, it's a natural extension of the previous step: "It sounds like you're having a hard time right now. I wonder if you're feeling overwhelmed by what's happened."

The challenge here is to remove as much of your own bias and expectation as possible, and be ready to abandon a guess if the other person tells you that's not in fact how they feel. It can actually be invalidating to have someone else incorrectly interpret your situation—as though they haven't heard you or have their own agenda. Use your knowledge of the other person as much as you can. Think about how they typically react to similar situations, or have responded to them in the past. It's likely that they have the same reaction now too. Some people do or say specific things when they're feeling various emotions. For example, some people speak in shorter sentences when they're upset. Notice cues like these and use them to read the other person's mind.

In level 4, we **frame the person's experience in their unique context**. This doesn't mean playing shrink and running wild with theories and assumptions, but seeing what you know about the other person as a whole. What's happened in their history to make this current situation more understandable? How does their unique life situation play into what they're telling you? You could acknowledge this context by saying something like, "Well, it makes sense that you would be overwhelmed by all this right now, since you've had so many big life changes lately."

Level 5 entails **normalizing reactions**. A big part of validation is knowing that you're not weird or wrong or bad, but having a perfectly normal and even common experience. "I'm sure anyone would feel stressed out if they had as much on their plate as you!"

Level 6, the final level, is about injecting some **radical genuineness**. This takes emotional acceptance deeper, and means we reach out on a personal level to the other person, emphasizing our shared human connection and experience. This is the level where you can reveal something about yourself, or become a little vulnerable—but whatever you do, it must be an *authentic* expression showing that you truly understand what the other person is telling you. However, you should be wary about not making the other person feel like you've hijacked the conversation and made it all about yourself.

As you can see, every situation will call for a different degree of validation—and it depends on *your* context and relationship with the person, too. Of course, you don't have to sit there and rigidly remember the six levels when a friend comes to you for support; rather, the takeaway from this model is to think of validation on a sliding scale—read the situation and dial up your level of validation accordingly.

How to Validate Someone — The Framework

Let's dig in even deeper. Validation is a kind of communication, and its purpose is to communicate acceptance. Let's take a look now at a step-by-step, detailed framework to follow when we want to provide validation. In reality, the six levels described above flow and blend into one another. There are different techniques, approaches and skills associated with each that, again, will vary in their effectiveness depending on the person you're talking to. Let's consider each in finer detail.

Step 1 – How to be present: listen!

No matter what the situation is, you should always go into it with an open mind and calm, focused attention on the other person. You are not coming in with an agenda. Rather, you are listening carefully to better understand their point of view, and their experience. This can actually be the hardest part, because when we care and want to help, we may want to jump in and start talking, offer advice, and so on.

But resist this urge in the beginning and let the other person take the lead. Let them speak and really listen. Here, your verbal communication is turned off for the most part, but your non-verbal communication comes to the fore.

Receptive body language: maintain an open posture and facial expression, and turn your body to face them. Relax. Make eye contact if it feels appropriate, but it's eye contact that is about interested, respectful attention rather than interrogation. Mirror their body language as closely as you can. If they're sitting with their legs crossed, do the same. If they have their arms resting on a table, you should too. Get rid of distractions—put your phone away, turn the TV off and show, with your body, "I'm here now, and I want to listen to what you have to say." It's also a good idea to match their tone and pace of speaking, as well as their "energy." If they are quiet and hesitant, for example, be quiet too, and tread carefully.

You might also encourage them to open up by asking, "Would you like to talk? I'm all ears." You might make encouraging "uh-huh" sounds or something similar, but at this step, silence can work wonders as an invitation for the other person to share.

Examples: Your roommate has just come home and clearly seems shaken up. Seeing this, you close your laptop and turn toward him, showing a concerned expression. He says he's just had a car accident and is feeling pretty stunned. Without saying too much (maybe a simple "tell me what happened"), you sit next to him and just listen without interrupting as he tells his story.

Or, imagine a woman tells her husband they need to talk. They sit down to chat, and she begins to explain something that's been bothering her, and that she's upset with him. Though it's tempting for the husband to respond immediately to what feels like accusations, he waits until she's said her piece.

Although he doesn't really like what he's hearing, he tries hard to just listen, and see things from her point of view, even though he would really like to share his own. When she's done talking, he pauses a little, so she doesn't feel as though he was simply waiting for her to shut up so he could jump in with a rebuttal!

Step 2 – How to reflect: ask questions

If the person simply wanted to be heard, and immediately feels better, you can sometimes stop at step 1. But you may find the conversation naturally shifts to your response to what you've heard. This is actively letting someone know you've heard them, because when you paraphrase what they've said, you are reflecting it back to them.

But when you reflect back, it only feels validating if it's *accurate*. The easiest way to do this is to literally repeat what you've heard. You can use reflection to summarize what's been said, to reiterate the most important parts of the story, or to distill some main essence of what they're feeling. For example, if somebody blurts out a long list of stressful events that have happened to them that day, you can say "Wow, it seems like there's so much going on right now."

Don't worry about your statement seeming overly obvious. When you reflect back, it's as though you are helping the other person tell their story. It lets them know that you're listening, and that you *get* it. It tells them that what they're expressing has actually landed, and communication is working.

Now, you don't have to jump in with clever-sounding guesses or tell them what they're feeling—if you don't know, you can always ask! Asking questions is further confirmation that you're listening and invested, and that what they say matters. Questions can prompt a person to keep sharing, and help them arrive at a more distinct conclusion themselves, in their own time.

Supportive questions:

"Okay, I want to understand what you mean when you say XYZ...can you tell me more?"

"So what did you think about that?"

"What do you think happens next?"

"Can you say more about XYZ?"

"So how are you feeling about all of this?"

Though it's not a bad question per se, avoid "so how does that make you feel?" as it can obviously feel a little cheesy!

Examples: If someone has just explained at length a complicated family drama, you may be a little confused on the details. Asking questions can show that you care about grasping the subtleties. "So, what's the relationship like between your mother and sister?" or "So you're worried that they had that discussion without you? Have I got that right?" Outright asking if you've understood correctly not only shows that you want to understand, but that you are centering the other person, which is validating in itself.

Questions are not just for your own clarification, though. You might well know how a particular story ends, but asking questions about it communicates encouragement and acceptance of the other person working their way through the story. "Okay, so then your mom told you about this conversation with your sister. What happened next?"

Questions and statements can both be used to achieve the same effect. Whether you frame it as an obvious question or more of a tentative statement, you are essentially asking, *Have I understood? Is this how it is for you?*

Step 3 – How to mindread: Use feeling words

If you spend a while in the previous step, you may find yourself naturally flowing into this step, where you speak more directly about the other person's experience. You began by listening and helping the person tell their story, and as you continue, it's as though you are helping them add more shape and structure to it. This makes sense when you think about it: when people are upset or emotional, they may not be thinking super clearly or rationally. They need to first express the emotions they're feeling, and only then find their way to processing and integrating the experience.

At this early stage though, try to avoid injecting your own interpretations into things. Think of yourself as a kind of guide or even midwife, helping a person get through their own experience, without making it too much about yourself. Sometimes, when people are upset, it can be helpful to put words to what they're feeling. Simply being able to say, "I'm feeling so disappointed right now" is a step toward acknowledging and owning your own experience.

"Mindreading" is perhaps a misleading word here, since you shouldn't really feel like you are guessing. But *tentatively* offer up an emotion word that might capture what they're going through. In doing so, you are helping people arrive at their own interpretations and conclusions. Naturally, you shouldn't just blurt out, "You're depressed" or flat-out tell someone how they're feeling.

Phrases to try:

"It seems to me like…"

"I'm wondering if XYZ is the case…"

"You seem quite angry/upset/scared/confused right now." (Said in a gentle, non-judgmental tone.)

"Do you think that made you feel XYZ?"

"I can see you're hurt."

"From what you're saying, it sounds like you're feeling XYZ about the whole thing."

Examples: Someone might be explaining at length the irritating things one of their friends does, giving a list of offenses, including the most recent one that caused a small argument. But in listening to them, you notice that they haven't actually stated outright how they feel. It might be obvious to you both, but you say, "Woah, seems like there's definitely a lot of frustration in this friendship."

By putting a single word to the collection of experiences, you not only show that you've listened, but that you can actually synthesize everything together, and see the bigger picture. This can really move a conversation along, and the other person might say, "Yes, that's exactly right. We seem to get *frustrated* with each other more and more lately..."

Though it's never your job to tell someone how they're feeling, they may get to see their emotions a lot more clearly when you reflect them back. If a different friend is complaining about how they're fed up with their girlfriend's male friends, you might say after a while, "I wonder if it's jealousy you're feeling?"

Even if you get the mindreading part wrong, so long as you're not being madly offensive, the other person is likely to appreciate the effort, and in correcting you, they are again engaged in sharing openly—a win-win situation.

Step 4 – How to find context: validate and center their experience

Again, one step may bleed over into the next, and asking questions or mindreading may easily lead to this step. At this stage, you want to communicate a strong sense of understanding who the person is, and how their experience is truly unique to them. You want to center them, and focus on their world and how it feels to be in it.

Here, you are still not offering your own interpretations, but rather helping the other person draw together their ideas so that they find their own conclusions themselves. We can absolutely provide validation to people we don't know that well, but more commonly, we know a little about them and their history.

When we validate and center another person, we are saying to them *your perspective is valid. This story and the way you're experiencing it makes sense.* For example, we can say, "I can totally see why you freaked out when that happened. Seeing as you've had bad experiences with this sort of thing in the past, it's not surprising you reacted the way you did."

We can bring in plenty of validation by acknowledging a person's unique perspective and history. This can make people feel really seen and heard. Some of the following phrases can be used alone to provide validation, but can also be extended and framed in terms of the person's context, or the broader situation.

Phrases that validate a person's unique experience:

"I can really see how the situation has made you feel this way."

"Given that you're a woman/Muslim/Australian/gymnast, I can understand why you responded as you did."

"What you say makes total sense to me."

"It's understandable that you feel like this."

"Well, you have a reason for feeling the way you do, and I completely understand that."

Example: If someone tells you they are struggling with PTSD after experiencing a violent crime, you can start by listening (being present), then ask them questions to flesh out their experience of the anxiety (so you can reflect). Then you might move on to saying something that vaguely summarizes their experience (mindreading, for example, "You've been under so much stress, I'm sure") and extend this by embedding it into the bigger context ("given what you've already been through, it's no surprise that you feel like this").

Step 5 – How to normalize: refrain from judgment

Judgment and acceptance cannot exist at the same time. When we validate people, we acknowledge that their experience is valid and their own, whatever it is. We can't do this properly if we have loads of criticisms or judgments about what *we* think of them. Maybe we don't agree with their appraisal of events. Maybe we think they're being foolish or missing something important. Maybe they're angry with us, and we want to defend ourselves. Or maybe we can't quite understand their response and it really does seem irrational to us.

Nevertheless, when we seek to normalize someone's experience, what we are really doing is telling them that it is *acceptable*, and that we don't judge them for what they're going through. You don't have to agree or share their opinion. You don't have to relate to the way they're telling their story or what they're choosing to focus on. But you can still communicate that *they* are entitled to feel that way, regardless of how your experience compares to theirs.

Many people have had the experience of reaching out to others for support, sympathy or (let's face it) a good old-fashioned rant, only to have their experience judged. They want to feel validated and heard, but instead, the other person might launch into a fact-finding mission, trying to root out who's to blame, and why, and what the logical and "correct" answer is.

Alternatively, some people may see the emotions of others as quite threatening, awkward or uncomfortable. Because they feel unable to validate and accept, for example, sad feelings in themselves, they react badly when they see them in others. Their response then is to judge. "Oh you're overreacting, it's not that bad" or "come on now, you're being a bummer, cheer up!"

When we normalize, however, we communicate that all feelings and all experiences are valid. Just because some feelings are uncomfortable or confronting, it doesn't mean that people are wrong for experiencing them. The other side of the coin, though, is that we can also be guilty of judging in the opposite direction, especially if we are trying to be supportive or helpful. When we say something like, "Oh it's so healthy that you're finally grieving that loss" or "you go girl, get mad!" we are also passing a value judgment on an experience.

We need to look beyond the specific emotion, thought or experience and to the person having it. We need to be able to say to that person: "It's OK to be who you are right now, and feel how you feel." Deep down, don't all of us want to know that we are not bad or wrong or strange? Don't we all feel a little better when we know that we're not the only people who feel the way we do?

Ways to express non-judgment and normalize:

"I think that most people would feel that way if they were in your shoes."

"It's totally normal that you feel like this."

"I would be upset too."

"There's nothing wrong with thinking these thoughts."

"You're not alone."

"Hey, I'm glad you told me how you feel." (normalizing the act of sharing)

Sometimes, the best way to show our acceptance and convey a sense of normalcy is not in the words we say, but in how we act, and what we *don't* say. Try to avoid making a pronouncement on what thoughts and feelings are good or bad. Don't comment on the strength or appropriateness of the feeling, for example, by suggesting an emotion is too much or too little. We'll look more at how *not* to validate in a later chapter.

Examples: A child reveals a rather shocking secret to their mother, but the mother is careful not to act horrified. By saying "I'm glad I know, you were right to tell me, and it's understandable that you're upset about this," she communicates both that the child's feelings are valid, and also that reaching out and sharing is welcome and acceptable—a profoundly reassuring position to take when someone is in distress.

Normalizing can be done briefly and as a matter of course, too. For example, someone shares something with their therapist and finishes with "but I'm sure you're used to seeing way more important problems in your practice." The therapist can respond, "Your problem *is* important. And many people come here with the very same concerns as you."

Step 6 – How to show genuine validation: Be real

When someone reaches out for help and support, the last thing they want is to feel like doing so makes them weak or wrong. When opening up to others, we all like to imagine that they understand a little about what we're saying, because they're human too, and have experienced suffering, loss, confusion, and other negative feelings. When the person listening can open up a little in return, we can feel immensely validated. We are not just being *told* we are OK and not alone—we actually experience it for real.

This final step of showing genuine human care and understanding is something that can't be faked. But one way to do it is to offer up something of your own experience. This isn't to derail the conversation or hog attention, but to confirm that you, too, know a little of what it feels like. "I lost my father last year, and I remember feeling that way, too."

Yes, it's always better to listen more and talk less, and you don't want to succumb to a preachy bit of advice or a story about how you did things better, but being a little vulnerable yourself can be a powerful thing to do. Don't share a story just to make a point or sneak in some advice—for example, "When my father died, I took up jogging. It was the only thing that kept me sane" (i.e. I think *you* should do the same). Rather, you are showing them that you are familiar with their emotion on a firsthand level.

We won't look at helpful phrases or examples here since the point of this step is to react genuinely, as the real person you are. Be honest. It can be as simple as saying

"I know how you feel," but, if you can truly *show* that you know, even better. "Did I ever tell you that the same thing happened to me last year?" And if you can't relate, it's probably better to just say that you can't, instead of trying to shoehorn your own experience in an attempt to match theirs.

As you can see, at no point in this process are you fixing any problems, offering any solutions, advice or suggestions, arguing, blaming, figuring out "the truth" or deciding whether the person's reactions are reasonable or not. You're also not trying to "help" by giving sagely words of wisdom or using your own experience as an inspiring example.

The above process may take an hour to unfold, with several loops back to previous stages. The person may need to dig deeper, rehash some things or tell the tale again before they're ready to move on or even ask for advice. Or, the process may be over in a minute, and not proceed all the way through. The way validation unfolds depends on just two things:

- The needs of the person receiving the validation

- The capacities, limits and skill of the person giving the validation

Takeaways

- Marsha Linehan has come up with a comprehensive, six-step model of validation that we can use when listening to others. Each step in this model relies on the previous one. One can't jump from step 1 to step 6; they must follow each step in the same order to validate someone in the best, most reassuring way possible.

- The first step in this model is simply being present. Here, you must actively listen to the other person and pay close attention. Give the other person subtle feedback through verbal and non-verbal cues which indicate that you're listening to them. This will make the other person feel more comfortable with you. The second step is called accurate reflection, and here you need to summarize what you've been told to provide further reassurance that you've understood what they've told you. Keep it simple, but significant.

- Next, try to read subtle cues the other person is giving. This involves some guesswork, but you only need enough information to be able to label their words with an emotion. For step four, try to contextualize the person's thoughts and emotions with either recent events from their life or past experiences which might be influencing their reaction.

- Step five is to simply reassure the other person that their reaction is reasonable and anyone else in their position would feel the same way. Lastly, for step six, you can relate their experiences with your own if you've been in a similar situation. Being vulnerable here can establish a stronger bond and invite further conversation and trust.

Chapter 3. Invalidation and Self-Validation

In speaking about validation, we've also inferred a little about its opposite. Not validating someone's experience, however, is seldom as blatant as "hey, your feelings suck, and you're not valid as a person!" In fact, invalidation is often done purely by accident, even by people deliberately trying to help. When we're on the receiving end of invalidation, we may even feel bad without knowing why—after all, wasn't the other person just trying to do the right thing?

Picture a group of friends, who notice that one of them is acting weird lately, turning down invitations and generally being a bit "off." It's burrito Wednesday and everyone usually gets together for some food and a chat, but the one friend, let's call him James, bows out and says he's not into it. The group decides to assemble at James's house this Wednesday, to cheer him up. While there, they can't help but ask what's wrong with him.

James explains he's been a bit down, and he's not up for socializing. He's upset about his recent breakup and is feeling like a bit of a failure in general right now. His friends, who think James is awesome, immediately jump in with encouragement.

"Don't say that about yourself! You're better off without her!"
"A failure? Come on man, it's not like you to say stuff like that."
"Chin up!"

They rally around him with praise and encouragement, despite James feeling more and more awkward. They decide to haul him out to a bar, to get some drinks, to get his mind off things. The advice flows thick and fast. "You need to hit the gym; you'll feel better in no time." "You need to get back out there on the dating scene." "You need more vitamin D, trust me."

It's obvious that at the end of the evening, James feels just as bad as before, if not worse. Though he was surrounded by caring, concerned friends, the effect was only that he was now painfully aware that he wasn't really allowed to feel how he felt, or express it. On top of his disappointment about the breakup, he now has an extra thing to feel bad about: his response to the breakup is an overreaction, uncomfortable, inconvenient. After all, why else would his friends do everything in their power to distract him and themselves from it?

On the other hand, James might have felt better if he had enough courage to set boundaries with his friends and communicate to them clearly that he felt how he felt, and that he didn't want to go out. If he was able to more clearly accept his own negative feelings, he might have been firmer in expressing them to his friends.

In this chapter, we'll be looking at invalidation from both sides of the coin— i.e. figuring out how we can be on guard against invalidating others, and also how we can overcome being invalidated ourselves. Connected to this is the idea of self-validation, or how we can avoid unconsciously invalidating our own experience.

What Is Invalidation?

Turning our original definition around, invalidation is when we see someone else's thoughts, feelings, experience or indeed their entire selves as invalid. Knowing how much every human needs to feel seen, accepted and acknowledged for who they are, invalidation can have profound effects. Invalidating someone gives them the sense that the experience they are having, the way they are feeling, their perspective, beliefs, preferences, boundaries and interpretations, are somehow *lacking*. With invalidation, we somehow feel that we are unreasonable, nonsensical, unwanted, not right, or just not important.

Everyone can be affected by invalidation, but children, who are still learning about who they are and how the world works, can be most profoundly impacted. If we are invalidated often and early on in life, we can have difficulty knowing who we really are, be unable to express or understand ourselves, or experience deep feelings of shame or self-doubt. When other people reflect and accept us, we feel solid; but when we are invalidated, our entire existence and self-worth can feel undermined. In fact, childhood invalidation may be at the heart of many mental health conditions and disorders.

This might sound dramatic, but constant invalidation can eventually lead to a deep feeling that you don't quite have the right to exist, or else that your existence is somehow fatally flawed and insignificant. In some cases, it can be used deliberately as a form of abuse. Validation is like a foundation to our identity, to our well-being, and our ability to connect meaningfully and communicate with others.

When this foundation is disturbed, it can have effects in all these areas.

We all know how it feels to be invalidated, but it can be tricky to spot exactly when it's happening. If we're used to it, we may even begin to think that it's normal. Invalidation can be dramatic or subtle, brief or ongoing, conscious or unconscious, and can play out in verbal and nonverbal ways.

Recognizing invalidation

Invalidation may not be done consciously. Many people invalidate others because they have been raised to accept invalidation as normal, or have been chronically invalidated themselves. They may be uncomfortable with emotions, or want to help but don't know how. On the other hand, some people do consciously invalidate the experience of a person they wish to control, as in gaslighting, where the other person is gradually taught not to trust their own accurate perceptions—i.e. they are made to feel crazy.

All invalidation shares a common core—it tells the other person "your experience is not valid." But there are different forms. For example:

Minimizing—"How can you be upset when other people have way worse problems?" "Oh, grow up, it's not really that big of a deal." "I'm sorry you feel that way." (Especially when it takes the place of an apology!)

Rejection—"That's the wrong approach." "Don't lower yourself to that level." "Only selfish people wallow like this."

Dismissing—"Oh, you'll get over it eventually." "It's nothing." "Ah yes, you're having a bit of a midlife crisis, huh? Join the club." Or simply being distracted when you talk and shrugging off what you say.

Denial—"I don't want to hear any more about this." "Come talk to me when you're ready to be rational." "That never happened/you never said that." Or simply pretending like they never heard what you said.

Controlling and judging—"You're being so over the top, you should calm down." "You're being dramatic again." "You don't make any sense." Or using the silent treatment.

Blaming—"Why do you always have to find a problem with everything?" "You've upset everyone again by saying that." "Well, I don't blame them for being mean to you, you do bring it out in people."

Though we've laid out a few different ways you can invalidate someone, the above categories can and do blur into one another, and there's no reason someone can't invalidate using every one of them. Nevertheless, it's obvious that any of these forms of invalidation can have horrible effects: people on the receiving end can feel alienated, worthless, and confused.

There are nonverbal ways to invalidate, too. If you roll your eyes, keep getting distracted by something else, pick at your nails like you're bored or offer any number of judgmental facial expressions, you don't have to say a word to send a message.

74

Invalidation can create conflict in relationships and erode trust, intimacy and communication. If you grow up in a household where your feelings are never seen, acknowledged or accepted, then it's going to be very difficult to be an adult who knows what they feel, can express themselves, be vulnerable, or acknowledge the emotions in others. In other words, *people who feel invalidated often go on to invalidate themselves and others.*

If you recognize some of the above in yourself, well done! It can be hard to acknowledge that we are not always doing our best to witness and support others. Sometimes, our cultures or workplaces can encourage invalidating behavior. For example, parents are told to minimize their children's feelings to help them toughen up or teach them a lesson, or workplaces may subtly punish honest expression and reward emotional bluntness.

Being a Good Communicator: How to Avoid Invalidating Others

Avoiding invalidating others is, in many ways, one of the first necessary steps to becoming good at validating them. The validation steps outlined in the previous chapter will undoubtedly convey kind, attentive acceptance to the person you're talking to, but you can imagine all that can go straight down the drain if you end the whole process with a comment like, "OK great, I'm glad you're done having your little breakdown now!"

Being a great communicator means being on guard for those times we might unconsciously invalidate others. Sadly, validation is not a skill people are taught directly, and we may have developed plenty of bad communication habits and assumptions that actually do quite a lot of harm when we engage with someone who is feeling vulnerable or distressed.

For example, a new mother might be expressing her extreme distress in the weeks after childbirth, and confide in a friend that she's having really dark thoughts. The friend, trying to reassure her, downplays the situation, but ends up invalidating her when she says something like, "That's just baby blues, don't you worry, it'll pass, I promise." The new mother is left feeling just as bad as before, but silly or ashamed for even bringing it up.

Or consider a doctor who is trying to put her nervous patient at ease by saying, "Don't worry, I've seen this all before, trust me...and it can be a lot worse than what you've got here." Instead of calming the patient, this comment makes him feel like his problem, as distressing as it is to him, isn't as important as other people's.

Similarly, we can cause enormous damage by invalidating *positive* emotions too. Consider someone who laughs at his friend's childlike excitement at going to a theme park and playfully teases him for being over the top, not realizing that his friend never had the experience in childhood, and that by telling him to calm down, he's made him feel ashamed for what could have been a positive moment.

In none of these examples are the people necessarily bad communicators, and they certainly don't have bad intentions. Nevertheless, to master validation means paying more attention to how we might be invalidating others anyway. We've explored all the validating methods to actively try, but now let's consider in detail what *not* to do.

Challenge 1: Undermining language

It's not what you say, it's the way that you say it! It's common to come across as invalidating when you assume that only the actual verbal content of your communication counts. But the way you speak, and the nonverbal message you send is just as (if not more) important. Think about how much tone of voice can change the statement, "Why did you do that?" Posture, facial expression, tone and gesture can change this statement from a gentle, curious inquiry to a full-blown accusation.

It's obvious that if we want to avoid invalidating others, we should refrain from using outright hostile language, name-calling, or negative words that make others feel bad. But we can also communicate invalidation subtly, for example by the indiscriminate use of the word "but." This tiny word has a way of cancelling out any positive expression that comes before it, and cementing the negative that comes after it. If you say, "That was great, but I'm wondering about page two," the other person might only hear "I'm unhappy about page two."

A good trick is to replace every "but" with "and" or simply cut it out entirely. "That was great! And I also had a few questions about page two." Sounds better, doesn't it? "But" is a word of contradiction. Think about any apology that goes, "I'm sorry, but..." It doesn't ever really feel like an apology!

To be more validating, it's also a good idea to avoid confrontational language, like addressing the person with "you" statements. These can feel provocative and even aggressive. Try to avoid telling people what they think or feel, e.g. "you're just tired right now" (even if you believe it's true!"). Eliminate words like *should*, *must*, *have to* and so on. You are not interested in what someone *should* feel or do—it's far more useful to talk about what they *actually* feel or have done. In the same way, words like *always*, *never*, *completely,* etc. can feel extreme and shut down conversation.

Use "I" statements to take responsibility for your own perspective and respect the other person's. There's a big difference between "you're confusing me" and "I'm confused." Avoid diagnosing someone, interpreting their actions, or explaining their experience to them. Share your own side, and invite them to share theirs without accusation, judgment or assumption.

Challenge 2: Judgmental attitudes

Nobody likes to think they're judgmental. On the other hand, a judgment occurs any time we look at something and appraise its value—hardly something we can avoid in life. When someone is talking to you, it can be a knee-jerk reaction to rush in with your own opinions and value judgments. In fact, human beings do this almost as a default, and often in more subtle ways than they know.

Firstly, when hearing someone talk, try to let go of the idea that it's your job (or anyone's) to figure out who's to blame, or decide on the "right" conclusion. For example, someone might be complaining to you about another person that insulted them, and you go into detective mode and try to see if an insult really was given, and how bad it was, and how much of a right the person has to be offended. When we put ourselves in the position of moral judge, we instantly turn off the option for empathetic and open-minded listening.

Fairy tales have villains and heroes, but most of the time, life doesn't. When people express themselves, they simply want to be heard, rather than strictly to be agreed with or told they're actually wrong. Those in positions of relative power might assume that it's their job to frame the story they hear and decide which reactions and feelings are correct, according to their own worldviews. This can be deeply invalidating for the person opening up and sharing.

We also end up imparting judgment when we decide on the correct *magnitude* of feelings or actions. When you express, consciously or unconsciously, that someone's experience is too much or too little, you are invalidating them. For example, by saying, "That's not such a big deal" or "you really need to be a bit more worried about this," you are passing judgment on the size and appropriateness of that person's emotions. But, it's never our right to tell people either *what* to feel, or *how much* of it to feel!

Challenge 3: Offering advice or going into fixing mode

We need to consistently remind ourselves of **why** people express themselves to us or seek our reassurance. It's seldom because they don't know how to fix the problem. It's because they want to be heard and validated, and to feel support for what they're going through. In other words, it's hardly ever a practical issue, but an emotional one. By offering practical advice, we leave the emotional need on the table, which can feel extremely invalidating.

Wanting to fix often comes from a good place, but can have the effect of making the other person feel invisible. Try not to ignore or minimize their feelings by rushing in with a solution. Chances are, they already *know* what to do and how to do it; they just need to be listened to, soothed, accepted or reassured.

Watch out for subtle ways of "fixing" such as asking, "Have you thought of XYZ?"—especially if XYZ is an obvious thing the person would have already considered. Avoid taking responsibility, and trying to make it your job to cheer the person up or solve all their problems. If you act as though the issue is a simple one that can be sorted out easily, you are in essence erasing the person's difficulties and struggles, as though to say, "If you could only see the solution as clearly as I can, then you wouldn't be so upset! Ta da!"

In the same way, advice is not a good idea unless it's explicitly asked for. Avoid things like, "If I were you..." or "what I usually do for this problem is..." The advice may seem relevant to you, but it might not feel that way to the other person. Remember, it's not about you—at all.

Challenge 4: Insincerity

Though we seldom think about it, there are culturally ingrained ways of soothing distressed people. We all have a mental model of what a good friend, or a kind mother, or a compassionate counsellor sounds like, and we might not even realize that we're defaulting to cliched expressions like, "How does that make you feel?" or "Shhh, it's going to be OK."

Though these stereotyped ways of responding to other people's emotions might have had genuine origins, the truth is that they often end up sounding insincere. Simply blurting out an automatic response or some truism that's supposed to be helpful usually doesn't actually help. Think of boring aphorisms like "time heals all wounds" or "you're stronger than you think!"

For validation to work, it has to feel real. The other person has to feel like they are having a genuine encounter with someone who really does understand and accept them, on a human level. How many people revert to what they think of as a kind, sympathetic voice, but which can sound to others incredibly condescending and irritating? A tilt of the head, an expression of "concern" and a fake-sounding "aw, how awful for you!" is likely to be received as an insult or brush-off rather than genuine care.

"You'll be OK, I promise" or "everything's going to be just fine" are empty phrases that not only fail to soothe, but tell the other person that you are not really listening, and don't have anything genuine to say. After all, how does anybody know how things will turn out? Even if the person will be OK in the future, what do they do with the fact that they don't feel OK *right now*?"

Overcoming Invalidation

We'll finish this chapter with a consideration of what to do if you yourself feel invalidated. As you might have noticed already, the reasons people invalidate one another are many, including simple carelessness. But one thing to remember is that *invalidation has nothing to do with the person receiving it*. It doesn't reflect on their worth as people.

The principle flowing through this entire book is that emotions, thoughts and lived experiences *cannot be wrong*. They are only what they are, and it is not for other people (or even for us) to decide they are not valid. If we feel invalidated, we might respond as though to an injury, and want to defend ourselves. We might double down in trying to make ourselves understood, or seek extra reassurance.

However, before you jump to react, ask yourself a few important questions to determine whether it's even worth it to try and reason with the person who has invalidated you. Ask yourself if the person is close to you, and whether they've made genuine attempts to understand you in the past. Is it really a good use of your time and energy to tell them they've invalidated you? Does their opinion even matter to you? Is this the right time to bring up their invalidation, or might it be perceived better if you did it later? If, after considering these questions, you believe it fit to respond, follow these steps:

1. First, don't accept the invalidation. Process what it feels like, but know it doesn't define you or your experience.

2. Communicate calmly and with "I" statements about how the invalidation has affected you.

3. Depending on the outcome of this, you can assert a boundary or choose to end the conversation entirely.

4. If you are routinely invalidated by someone, it might be time to consider the value that relationship holds in your life.

The important thing to remember here is that you must not get into a debate about whether their invalidation or your desire for validation is right or wrong. You are merely establishing a boundary about how you want to be treated. What the boundary should be is entirely up to you and can vary based on how exactly you were invalidated.

In learning how to validate others, we ourselves become better at asserting our own confidence and boundaries. Use mantras or mottos (like "all feelings are valid") to remind yourself that you have a right to your experience. You can never demand that people praise, like or agree with you, but you can expect respect, and you are always allowed to walk away from relationships where your genuine experience is not respected.

The path to self-validation

It's far easier to manage being invalidated if you have your own strong inner sense of confidence and self-worth. If you are in the habit of undermining your own experience, it's likely you will not be able to defend against the same from other people, and you may even invite it. Self-validation is an act of compassion for yourself. It is constantly confirming for yourself, "I matter as much as anyone else, and my perspective is valid. My thoughts, feelings and emotions are mine and are not wrong. No matter what others say, I have belief and respect in myself." What a powerful attitude!

There are several ways you can validate yourself. Affirmations are one great way wherein you repeat certain prewritten lines or passages to yourself. You can find some great ones online or write one for yourself. Take note of all the negative thoughts that enter your brain when you're invalidated, and then write down the things you wish someone else would've said to you to soothe those worries. In addition to using affirmations, you can also maintain a daily journal where you practice gratitude and appreciate the good things you did on any particular day.

This helps foster a third way to self-validate, which is practicing positive self-talk. When you cultivate this habit, you don't need to have a journal with you. You will be able to reassure yourself amidst whatever issue you're facing. It's easy to gloss over our strengths and disproportionately focus on weaknesses, but this habit can be overcome with practice and discipline.

You can also use Linehan's six-step model for validation on yourself. Nothing in any of the steps necessitates another person carrying them out. You can be mindful of your own emotions, reason with them, contextualize your reaction within the broader scheme of events in your life, reassure yourself that others might react similarly, and recount instances where other people you know have faced similar problems as you. These need not be friends or family; it can be anyone.

Real maturity comes when we are able to tolerate disagreement and conflict, when we are able to see that people don't share our perspective, but can nevertheless value that difference and affirm its validity anyway, for ourselves and for others. Listening compassionately and with respect doesn't mean you'll automatically agree. But when you are confident and secure in your own self-worth, you may find that you seek out validation far less, and are much more ready to offer it to others.

Every human being has an emotional life and inner experience that is completely their own, and which they are entitled to. When it comes to the validity of others and our own validity, we cannot help but support one when we support the other. In an argument, for example, two people who are secure in the validity of their own experience will be able to reach a resolution far quicker.

They can both say to each other, "I can see what it's like to be you, and I'm glad you can see what it's like to be me. Neither of us is wrong. Even if we disagree, we are still valid people and our experiences are still real, important and deserving of respect." Can you imagine how difficult it would be to have a serious conflict if both people felt this way?

Takeaways

- Invalidation is doing or saying anything that makes another person feel that their thoughts, emotions, or even their entire sense of self are wrong and unreasonable. People who have been regularly invalidated during childhood develop severe mental and emotional issues in their adult life. They are at risk of developing mental health disorders, practicing invalidating behaviors themselves, having a weak sense of self, constantly doubting themselves, and so on.

- People who invalidate others generally do so for two reasons. First, they intend well but simply don't know the best way to validate someone else. So, they end up engaging in either minimizing, judging, or denying the other's issues. However, there is also another group of people who intentionally invalidate others, such as in the form of gaslighting. Here, people train others to doubt their own sense of perception about things by continuously invalidating them.

- Some of the most common ways in which we might invalidate others include using undermining language, having judgmental attitudes, trying to fix another person's problems when they just want to be heard, etc. Avoid using words like "but" by replacing them with "and" while also being mindful of your tone while conversing. Don't exercise judgement and remember that you are not being asked for a solution, the other person simply wants their thoughts to be heard.

- When someone invalidates you, it's essential to establish clear boundaries, especially if the other person is close to you. If not, you may simply choose to end the conversation and cease contact. But if they are close, you'll want to calmly use "I" statements to convey how the invalidation made you feel and set boundaries that establish how you want to be treated in the future.

- When another person doesn't give you the validation you wanted, practice self-validation. Use affirmations, journaling, practice positive self-talk, or you can even use Linehan's six-step model by yourself. All of these practices help you become self-sufficient and less dependent on others to affirm your thoughts and emotions.

Chapter 4. Validation and Conflicts

A: "I feel like you're always criticizing me…"

B: "What are you talking about? I never criticized you!"

A: "I know you don't *mean* to, but that's what it feels like."

B: "Well, what did I say? I'll take it back."

A: "It's not about what you said…"

B: "Well, I don't know what you want—do I have to apologize for something I never did?"

In this chapter, let's delve a little deeper into what validation (and self-validation) really looks like in the real world, where messy conflicts are possible. Though it's not too difficult to understand and sympathize with someone who is feeling upset, it's a different story entirely when they're upset with *us*. And though we can acknowledge that someone has a right to their own perspective, it can be very difficult to know what to do when that perspective directly threatens our own.

We've already mentioned that validation is not the same as agreement. When we validate someone, we are not saying their claims or assessments are *true* or that we like them, only that they are in their rights to feel what they feel. Validation is an excellent tool to help people who are distressed, to become a better listener, a more supportive friend, and so on. But perhaps it shows its best colors in more difficult situations, i.e. when people disagree, or there is outright aggression or hostility. Validation is a powerful tool for dealing with heated disagreements, misunderstandings, arguments or oppositions—like the one above.

Validation Is Not Agreement

Maybe in reading the previous chapters, you've thought, "That all sounds great, but what about talking to a person who is clearly mistaken/insulting/crazy/just plain wrong? Surely there's no real way to validate something like that?"

We should begin with a fundamental principle: **validation is not about ideas, thoughts or feelings. It's about people**. When we validate someone, we are acknowledging their right to be as they are, regardless of the details. *We want to offer emotional, and not informational validation.* So, in theory, it doesn't matter how bizarre someone's perspective is or how wrong we think they are. Of course, in practice, it's another story...

Let's say you are being told a story where someone feels disrespected, when you know for a fact that they were not. Or you hear about someone's anger but, in your opinion, it's they who are in the wrong and you can't help but side with the other person. Compare the following responses to someone who's feeling insulted:

A: "You're right. That other person is definitely an idiot."

B: "Hey, I honestly don't think they meant to offend you."

C: "I can understand that you feel slighted, given what you've told me."

Though response A is technically agreement, it's actually no better than response B, since both of them are not validating the emotion so much as the content. Only C offers validation for the person's experience, separate from whether they're right or wrong about being insulted. Let's look at an even more difficult example, and something many people have trouble with: offering validation to someone whose perspective is seen as utterly wrong or even in opposition to their own.

"It's obvious the world is being manipulated by a race of evil reptilians who can shape shift."

Non-validating response: "Uh... come on, you don't really believe that nonsense, do you?"

Validating response: "Wow. It seems like the whole idea terrifies you…"

"Women were so much happier in the '50s because they knew their place!"

Non-validating response: "[a string of expletives]"

Validating response: "Hmm. Growing up in the '50s yourself, I can see why you'd feel that way."

"You're just a therapist, you only pretend you care because people pay you."

Non-validating response: "You're just projecting."

Validating response: "I can tell you're angry at me right now. I also think you know that when you say that, it really hurts me."

As you can see, validation is possible even when we feel the other person is being downright irrational or offensive. In the third example, the therapist openly acknowledges disagreement and offense, while still noting and respecting the other person's feelings. We can always strive to communicate that the other person has every permission to feel how they do (i.e. validate them) while still asserting our own boundaries and know that *we* can feel how we feel, too (self-validation).

We can always say something that recognizes that, given that person's history and perspective, they would feel what they feel. It can sometimes feel harder to offer acceptance and acknowledgement to those we disagree with because we don't want them to think they're right, or we don't want them to feel that we are complicit in their actions or beliefs. But we simply need to remind ourselves that we don't have to agree with them—ever. We can offer understanding, respect and consideration all without ever changing our opinion, or theirs.

If you can do this, however, don't be surprised if other people's strange opinions start to seem less strange after a while, and that they, after feeling heard and respected by you, are far more willing to listen to your side of things. Arguments and misunderstandings often dissolve when people can genuinely put aside their preconceptions (yes, you included) and try to really hear what the other person is saying.

Look beyond the plain information they're sharing and see the emotional content. How can you respect their experience, and have compassion by putting yourself in their shoes? If we look honestly, below the surface details, we can see that humans are emotional beings. When we acknowledge and affirm one another's sincere emotional realities, it can have the effect of melting disagreements "out there" in the world. It can be very freeing to realize that you can always offer this to another person, whether you can relate to them or not.

Does practicing validation mean you can never correct obvious misinformation or call out thinking or attitudes that can genuinely harm others? Of course not. But all of this can be done *in addition to* offering emotional validation. For example, "I can tell you're really upset at the idea that everyone was laughing at you. I can imagine how anxious that makes you feel, given that people have been unkind to you before. I also wonder if you know that, truthfully, they really weren't laughing at you?"

Let's return to the conversation we began with:

A: "I feel like you're always criticizing me..."
B: "Really? Oh no. It wasn't my intention to criticize you."
A: "I know you don't *mean* to, but that's what it feels like."
B: "Oh wow. I can see this has really upset you. I'm sorry you feel criticized." **(Notice— validation occurs without necessarily agreeing with A.)**
A: "Aw, thanks, to be honest it's not really you, I can be overly sensitive sometimes..."

Validating Amidst Disagreement

A funny thing happens when we routinely practice validation: we start to realize that disagreement is not really such a big problem. It is possible to disagree with someone without being disagreeable, and you can still actively validate others and yourself even as you actively question their viewpoints. Though this all sounds nice in theory, how do we actually get it done in real life?

Using validation can be difficult in a world that seems built on division and hostility. It seems that today you can't take a step in any direction before seeing difference of opinion leading to hostility and vicious conflict. But, whoever we are, we can always lead by example and practice civility.

Three Rules for respectful, tactful disagreement

- Start by trying to **understand the other person's point of view**

before trying to get them to understand yours. Begin interaction with an open mind, and actively set aside expectations, biases and prejudices. Before you get defensive and shut down, really listen to what the other person is saying with validation, and without judgment.

- **Focus on people, not ideas.** People are not their views. When you disagree, you disagree with an idea or concept, and not with the person who holds that idea. Beliefs can change; but people are always worthy of respect and understanding. Another way of stating this is that relationships are almost always more important than winning arguments. It is perfectly possible to hold a person in high regard while disagreeing with what they think.

- **Look for commonalities**. People always have more in common than they first think. Even if you differ, aren't you both human beings, and don't you both share in the fundamental experiences of life? Instead of choosing to see others as enemies, deliberately find ways to connect with them in friendship and understanding. You could even bond over the fact that you both are sharing a frustrating disagreement!

When people look at others primarily in terms of the content of their thoughts and opinions, they can lose sight of them as *people*, who have an inner world and an emotional reality that is as real and as valid as their own. So, instead of seeing people as people, we see them as members of different races or ethnicities, nationalities, political parties, demographics, generations or religious groups. And when we see them that way, we can't help but conceive of ourselves the same way, in opposition to them. We start to frame things in terms of "us vs. them" and completely forget that people have arrived at their worldviews and perspectives in exactly the same way as we have.

Many people like to think of themselves as compassionate, empathetic souls who are amazingly open-minded...but of course the catch is that they only feel they should behave this way to others who already agree with them! In the wake of the Covid-19 fallout and the worsening divisions all around the world, it's easier than ever to assume that those who disagree with us are not only wrong, but are completely, utterly contemptible and more or less deserve to die.

Closer to home, individuals can find that global political tensions and controversies filter into their personal relationships. A couple might have a very serious fight about the #MeToo movement, or a family might feel they can't eat dinner at the same table because it could lead to a shouting match over politics. Friends might end friendships because they disagree on climate change, or some other hot-button topic that sharply divides opinion. Does genuine validation have a place in a world so full of contention and discord?

Let's remember that the point of validation is to provide the person we're listening to with the sense that they are seen, heard, acknowledged and accepted. And this is something we need and crave too! Though our knee-jerk reaction to ideas we don't like might be to resist, to get aggressive or to ignore, we always have in our power the ability to validate someone's (and our own) emotional reality.

Changing the goal of interaction

Arguments and hostility can arise when, consciously or unconsciously, we hold the following goals in conversation:

- To be right

- To convince others to think as we do

- To feel superior

- To find out "the truth"

- To punish people who are wrong or stupid

- To defend against anyone who is attacking our beliefs

- To prove something

However, we can completely change the way we engage with others when we change our approach, and have just one goal:

- To see and be seen, to understand and be understood

The first set of goals is all about the content, whereas the second goal is simply to work at the level of individual validation and respect. When we validate others, we bypass theories and ideas and arguments, and get to the root: we connect with them as people, and communicate that their inner reality is acceptable, important, and seen.

When people argue about the big scary topics (religion, sex, politics and so on), they often get embroiled in hostility because they don't feel seen or understood. They react defensively, and behave in ways that make it so that they can't see or understand the other person's point of view, either. Not being seen or appreciated can feel like a threat—one that we respond to by threatening others in the same way. It's a vicious cycle.

Ask yourself:

Can you see how the other person has arrived at their viewpoint?

Does any part of it make sense to you?

Can you see how their core values are reflected in how they're behaving and what they're saying?

Are there positive things you can both agree on?

Remember, in using validation, we are not trying to see whether we agree or not, but whether we can look at someone who's different from us and say "I see you. I understand." If you doubt the power of doing this for others, try to imagine for a moment the effect these words might have on you when heard from someone you assumed to be your complete enemy.

Genuinely saying "I don't agree with you, but I see where you're coming from and can respect that" can be a powerful way to heal division and connect people. When approached this way, dialogue is possible. You can begin to ask questions to better understand the other side, and try to explain your own point of view. Again, this is not to persuade or lecture, but to aid in understanding.

Disagreements in life are unavoidable. But we always have a choice in how we respond to difference. No single perspective is "right" or better than any other, and genuine respectful conversation can widen everyone's scope rather than narrow it. Before we move on, here are some questions to consider when you encounter friction in daily life:

- Is this problem really worth disagreeing over? Do you lose anything by letting it go?

- What are your own values and boundaries on this issue? What are your responsibilities in communicating them?

- What are your personal blind spots, biases, expectations and flaws when it comes to this issue? What could you learn?

- Is your verbal and nonverbal communication conveying acceptance?

- Are you being respectful, and have you tried to find common ground?

If you have sincerely done your best with someone you don't agree with, then it doesn't mean you can't walk away when things don't improve. One person cannot have a validating, respectful conversation all on their own—you might still need to draw a line and say, "We don't see eye to eye on this, that's fine, but I'm stopping the conversation here." Don't apologize for holding a different opinion, or asserting a boundary. You might find that sometimes, honest disagreement is the first moment of real sincerity of the whole discussion!

Validation Even in Conflict

We'll end our chapter on the trickiest part of using validation during conflict: those occasions when the other person is angry *at you*. Here, you need a careful strategy. It can be quite difficult to affirm someone's negative perception of you while still wishing it weren't true, even (especially?) when their criticism happens to be accurate.

But we can *always* affirm and accept other people's perspectives, even if we find ourselves inside that perspective, and not exactly in the most flattering light! It comes down to carefully balancing validation of others with self-validation, or hearing their complaint against you with compassion and acceptance, without being a pushover or taking a dent to your self-esteem. We can show respect for others while holding our own ground. More than that, we can genuinely learn and be better people without succumbing to blame games and accusations.

It's key to understand that validation in this circumstance actually *helps you*—you get over conflicts faster, and you have more chance of being seen and understood yourself. You can also use what they've told you to become a better person by working on areas they've criticized if you believe that there is any merit in their statements. It really is a win-win. If we consider people's history, their perceptions, their personality, and so on, then their emotional reality **always does make sense**. And this is true even if they're mad at you or making accusations that aren't fair.

Remember that our goal is not to win arguments, to beat the other person, to feel superior or root out the facts. Rather, the goal is to see and be seen. So, the question becomes, how can you maintain your own boundaries and validate your position while simultaneously validating the other person's?

This is why self-validation can make it easier to validate others—we can **share** the feeling of being heard, of being important, or being seen and understood. We are already united when we work together at achieving this for both of us. Here are some steps to follow that draw on the validation techniques we've already covered, with some additional strategies.

Step 1: Always start by listening, being present and opening your mind. Don't retaliate or interrupt. You'll have your chance to speak later.

Step 2: Reflect what you've heard by paraphrasing or asking questions. Talk about emotions here, and not factual data. Be mindful of your choice of words, tone, and body language. Any indication that you've taken offense will immediately make the other person defensive and potentially escalate the argument. This is especially important if the conversation is not happening face-to-face. Remember, you are seeking first to understand, before you make yourself understood. You are not sizing up the feelings they're sharing, just appreciating what they are.

Step 3: Accept responsibility. You can validate someone's accusations when you plainly and neutrally accept that they may be right. You don't have to accept all of it, but be honest. You are not arguing, or defending, or finding something to accuse them of. You are just owning what rightly belongs to you. Note that you don't have to agree with the content, but the emotion underneath it. If someone accuses you of snubbing them, you can acknowledge that you've been a little distracted lately without agreeing that you deliberately set out to insult them.

Step 4: Assert your own side of things. Here is the main balancing act. Calmly and neutrally assert your own boundaries (if necessary) and try to share what your experience has been. Beware, though, that this will only be heard if the other person feels that you've already acknowledged their side. Use non-confrontational, "I"-focused language and avoid explanations that sound like excuses or arguments. Here, you are simply sharing your own emotional reality—which is also valid. You may need to go through steps 1 to 4 a few times before you reach a resolution.

Step 5: If it feels right, close off the argument with more validation. Use "we" language to emphasize that it is "us versus the problem, rather than me versus you." Thank the person for sharing their concerns with you, and for listening to you in return.

Even conflict can be useful if it strengthens connections between people.

Now, granted, all of this can sound a little too good to be true. Arguments can sometimes go sour even if you do your best to validate. And sometimes, issues need more than one discussion to be properly hashed out. You might find that people's anger makes them unable to hear you or offer much compassion, especially if they feel wronged by you. They may reject any attempt you make to reconcile or discuss, and seem only to want to make you feel bad in retaliation.

In this case, avoid the temptation to turn things around and get angry at them. Instead, own your responsibilities quickly and happily, assert your boundaries, and move on. When we practice validation and self-validation together, we can always balance respect and compassion for ourselves with the same for others.

Takeaways

- It's one thing to validate someone when their grievances are aimed at someone else. It's another thing entirely to do so when you are the source of their frustrations. Another challenging scenario is validating someone when they're espousing views or thoughts that are morally abhorrent to you. However, in both these cases, it is essential that we focus on the person and not the content of their argument. Always remember that validation is not agreement; you can validate without accepting someone's views.

- There are three easy steps you can follow when trying to validate someone voicing objectionable statements. First, try to understand their emotions and viewpoint before attempting to get your own point across. Second, focus on the person, what they're going through and where they're coming from before judging. Third, focus and try to find commonalities between you two. Even when it seems like there aren't any, there likely are. You just need to avoid being so turned off by the conversation that you stop looking.

- It's easy to feel like you're doing something wrong by validating someone who says things you find disturbing or even horrifying, but it's important to keep in mind that validating does not mean agreeing. It's essential that we acknowledge everyone has an inner emotional reality that is valid in its own way and we have no right to judge them for it, especially when we haven't taken the time and effort to understand them properly.

- Validating someone who is mad at you is a subtle but highly useful skill. The main way to do this is to keep reminding yourself that the point is not to win any arguments and not to establish your superiority over the other. You are merely allowing the person to express and have their emotions accepted even if you don't agree with them. Listen to them attentively, accept responsibility for your actions, offer your side of things calmly and without invalidating what's been said, and end the conversation with further validation and framing the issue as a "we" problem rather than a "me vs. you" one.

Chapter 5. Empathy: Beyond Validation

If you keep butting heads with someone in your workplace, you can eventually reach a point where you say to one another, "Look, we don't agree, but that's fine. I see where you're coming from, and to some extent it makes sense to me. I don't like your opinion, but I do get it." That would be satisfactory, and you would probably get along well enough in the office to move past your differences with respect and tact. Nobody would expect you to have a rich and deep understanding of your colleague's inner world and respect it on a human level—in fact, it would be a little weird! It's simply enough to be civil.

I'm sure you can see, however, that "agreeing to disagree" wouldn't work nearly as well in, say, a marriage or the relationship between parent and child. Can you imagine a husband saying to his wife in couples' counselling, "Hey, whatever, you do you"? Probably not! This is because, while validation is great, it doesn't necessarily reach the level of genuine empathy. And it's genuine empathy that's essential in close, personal relationships.

We've seen that validation differs from empathy. With validation, we recognize that another person's experience is inherently valid. With empathy, though, we *feel* that world for ourselves, from the inside out. Let's take a closer look.

Validation vis-a-vis Empathy

What is empathy? When we are aware of and can relate to someone's emotional reality, we are empathetic. We can practice validation and respect even when we don't quite understand the emotions of the person in front of us. So, it is possible to validate someone's experience without necessarily having empathy for it. However, when we have empathy, it's much easier to validate other people, and indeed, the concepts do overlap.

Validation is to acknowledge the validity of the inner world of another person, whereas with empathy we *enter into that world*.

With empathy, we understand people beyond the intellectual. We see them as they really are, rather than as *we* are, or as we wish them to be. We can see and know their suffering, because we, too, have suffered. We can hear them and understand their point of view as they themselves see it. Empathy and compassion are very close— because if we know how someone feels, we almost certainly regard them with kindness.

Empathy can take a few different forms, and focus either on cognitive empathy (understanding someone else's thoughts and intellectual world), or emotional empathy (understanding their feelings). But empathy in general is used to talk about any sensation we have where we can set aside our own perspective and priorities, and see into another person's. With empathy, we look at others and hold compassionate feelings for the fact that their experience is so totally different from ours, and yet still worthy of love and respect.

With validation, we let the other person know that their world *makes sense* to us, that their experience is understandable and their feelings are valid. Empathy requires sinking deeply into those feelings and experiences, to see what they're like from that person's point of view.

Now, the point here is not to dwell on all the minute differences and similarities between these obviously related ideas. The goal is to see that they are distinct, and can be used to different effect in different situations and with different people. For example:

"I'm really upset that I didn't pass my driver's test."

"Oh, I'm sorry to hear that. It makes sense you'd be upset, I know how hard you studied for it!" **(This response shows validation—"your feeling makes** sense"—yet there isn't necessarily any empathy in it.)

"I'm really upset that I didn't pass my driver's test."

"I failed my test too. I didn't cry about it though, I just booked to take it again, no big deal." **(This response shows empathy but not much validation.)**

"I'm really upset that I didn't pass my driver's test."

"Oh, I'm sorry to hear that. It makes sense you'd be upset, I know how hard you studied for it! I failed my test the first time too, and it sucked, so I get it." **(This response shows validation and empathy, because a shared connection is made.)**

As mentioned, the best response will depend heavily on the person you're talking to, your relationship with them, what they really need from you, and the topic at hand. It's hard to imagine any situation where validation might not be appreciated; however, validation + empathy is typically more appropriate in closer personal relationships.

What about empathy on its own? Well, imagine sharing some devastating news with someone, who proceeds to be as devastated as you, since it reminds them of having to deal with the same thing. You might feel the other person's empathy (they know how you feel) without strictly feeling validated (i.e. that the response is understandable and valid).

Developing Empathy

Most of us want to be empathetic people, but good intentions are not always enough. Fortunately, it's always possible to cultivate empathy in yourself, and practice definitely makes perfect. There are many resources and models out there, but when it comes down to it, empathy is pretty simple in practice. To empathize, we need to be open-minded and accepting enough to enter into someone else's world, and we must be able to communicate our acceptance of this world to them.

Using this definition, there are three key parts we can focus on to make sure we're doing our best to empathize:

1. We need to be open-minded, receptive and accepting

2. So that we can enter into another person's world

3. And then communicate this understanding and acceptance to them.

Empathy won't quite be complete unless it contains all three elements, so it's worth trying to hit each note when you're having a conversation with someone and want to go beyond validation. Let's look closer.

Element 1: Open-mindedness

Perhaps it would be better to say, "open-heartedness."

As we saw in the six-step validation process earlier, it all starts with receptive, respectful listening. We can only empathize with others if we take the time to set aside our own ego for a moment, and actually pay attention to someone else. This openness is a special attitude characterized by being deeply present with what is, and being willing to learn something new.

In a way, it's a loving curiosity about other people in the world—the desire to know more about people and what makes them tick. The best way to do this is to forget about yourself for a moment. Get out of your world and set aside your assumptions and biases. Look at other people like they are fascinating books waiting to be read, or new planets waiting to be explored. Drop the idea that people should be characterized as friend or foe, or judged according to how much they agree with you. Rather, see people on their terms entirely. Another person is a whole new universe—see yourself as an adventurer exploring these new realms with respect and awe.

Practically speaking, what this looks like is occasionally stepping out of your comfort zone: engage with people, ideas and media you ordinarily wouldn't, just to see what happens. This will help you reveal and work on your biases, something all of us have in some form. Due to how homogenous our social circles have become, we're often closed off or ignorant of how other people see the world around us and how their perspective contrasts with our own views. Have a conversation where you just shup up and listen, making the other person the complete focus of your attention. Travel, if you can, or simply go somewhere different from where you normally go. Turn on all your senses and really open up to experiences different from your own.

But we are not just opening to positive feelings: can you imagine what it must be like to have difficulty with something that you currently experience as easy or automatic? Go without a luxury for a while. Humility is a great friend of empathy. The next time you are disappointed, angry, confused or sad, sit with the feeling for a moment and try to imagine others who have been there. Try on all perspectives, including those where you feel helpless and vulnerable. What a wonderful resource to draw on the next time you encounter someone who feels that way!

It might be nice to think of empathy as something inborn, a bit like a personality trait, but in reality it's a muscle we can exercise, and a skill we can develop if we really want to. Simply knowing this already makes us more receptive and open-minded. You can ask yourself earnestly, in what ways could I be more empathetic, right now? What is really standing in the way of me fully entering into the world of another person?

You can practice open-mindedness right now. Think of someone in your life, preferably someone you have a little friction with, or perhaps have had difficulty empathizing with in the past, then ask yourself:

How are they feeling right now? What is their behavior like, and what do they say and express? In other words, what must it be like to be them?

If you can identify their emotions, ask yourself why they might be responding that way. Can you see how the facts of their personalities, histories, strengths, weaknesses, etc. have contributed to their experience? You are really asking—in what ways does their reality make sense to you?

Can you find any points of commonality between you both? Have you felt like this person before? If not, can you imagine how it might feel to be in their shoes?

Element 2: Walking in their shoes

Empathy is not just abstractly understanding that someone else lives in a different world from you, or looking at it from afar with detached interest. Rather, empathy is "walking in their shoes" and seeing that world through their eyes. This is important—you don't regard the facts of their experience from your own perspective, but from theirs. This takes you deeper than mere validation. You not only see, acknowledge and respect the difference, but embrace it and engage with it as your own (albeit temporarily).

Once we have truly listened and heard another's experience, once we have been receptive to what it's like to be them, we can try on that perspective for ourselves.

We can feel their feelings, think their thoughts. Obviously, empathy is an intimate act, and it isn't really possible or even desirable to maintain this state of mind for prolonged periods. When we develop empathy, we need to remain conscious of deliberately seeing into another life, while still maintaining our own sense of self and the boundaries around it.

Generally, we can get better at walking in someone else's shoes the more we do it. This means when someone tells us something, we don't just accept it and move on; we ask questions so we can understand the person, deeply. *Why* do certain things matter to this person? How do they feel about XYZ, and how do their core values and beliefs all fit together?

How do they explain life to themselves, what language do they use, what do they focus on, and what is their attitude? Importantly, you are seeing their world *as they see it*, not as you do. You might not agree or understand it at all, from your perspective. But can you see that from their perspective, their world makes perfect sense, and everything is in order when you change your frame of reference?

Practically, a great way to develop this skill is perhaps an unexpected one: read. When you read fiction, you are asked to imagine life from a character's point of view. You suspend your own identity for a while and look at the world from their identity instead. This is not dissimilar from what you do when you empathically imagine another person's reality. Your world may be a rom-com, but what must it be like to be the protagonist in a sci-fi spy novel set 3000 years in the future?

Some questions to ask yourself to get into the mind of another:

What are their core values? How do they manifest?

How do I appear to this other person?

What matters to this person? What hurts them and what fulfills them?

What are this person's goals in life?

How does this person think of themselves? (This can be illuminating—few of us can say our self-conception matches the general impression we make to others!)

Element 3: Communicating acceptance

The final part of the empathic process is to bring your new sense of understanding and acceptance into the real world, and share it with the other person. You could have complete empathy for their thoughts and feelings, and sincerely see where they're coming from. But if you *do nothing* about it, and cannot share that you have this knowledge, its's almost as though you didn't have it. Empathy is its most powerful when it can be demonstrated to the object of its focus, and when it can power our behavior in the real world.

In this final and perhaps most important aspect of empathy, we need to take our feelings of validation and acceptance, and convey them meaningfully to the other person. We need to allow our enriched understanding to benefit not just them as individuals, but to enhance our relationships and deepen connection and understanding.

133

What does this look like practically? In reading this book, and learning ways to alter techniques such as communication styles, you have already taken a step in this direction. When we take active measures to become better listeners, to express acceptance for others, and to *show* what empathy looks like in the real world by modeling it during disagreements and arguments, we make empathy practical.

The question is, once you have opened yourself to another's experience, and once you have stepped into it with respect and acceptance, how can you communicate it?

We can choose compassionate and careful language that shows our respect and understanding. We can share something of ourselves, so when we say "I understand" it seems like more than just words. We can ask insightful and thoughtful questions that show we are listening. We can remember the things that are shared with us. We can respect boundaries when they're asserted, and take responsibility for times when we miss the mark. All these things are not just about caring, but *showing* you care.

Finally, something you might not have considered is that it is, in a way, our duty to others to be compassionate with ourselves. When we learn to self-validate, we become experts, and we can then take that mastery to others, bringing acceptance and validation to them. When we love and care for ourselves, we elevate all our relationships and interactions, and inspire others to self-validate, too. Empathy is not just a nice idea; it's something we **do**, practically, every day.

Once you've done the work of generating empathetic and validating feelings, put them to work, and ask the following questions:

What does this person most need right now?

In what ways am I contributing to how they feel, and what part of the situation is my responsibility?

Have I been honest and open in expressing how I feel?

Have I set my own boundaries clearly, and am I respecting other people's?

What could I say or do right now that would improve the situation?

Have I fully expressed my acceptance and openness to this person—in terms and language they will understand?

If you read more widely on the topic of empathy, you might find that all its different aspects are some version of one or more of the above three elements (the six-step validation process is an example).

We can understand each element as a progressive step, a process that starts within us and brings us closer and closer to others. Empathy begins inside us (1), then makes a bridge to another person (2), and eventually rests fully with them when we express our empathy (3). You may discover, in trying to practice, that you are better at one element than the other. Great! This can help you focus your efforts.

Let's look at an example that uses all three elements. Let's say Peter has a friend, Mike, who has wildly different political views from him. Because he values Mike's friendship, and because he wants to be a more empathetic, understanding person in general, Peter decides to change his approach to the usual disagreements between the two.

Privately, Peter gets to learning more about Mike's viewpoint. He reads unfamiliar news sources, and tries to really understand the arguments being made. He suspends his own judgment and tries to look with open eyes. Can he see the elements in Mike's life that make these arguments appealing to him? As he reads and researches, he realizes something: Mike is a deeply principled and passionate person, who really only wants to do the right thing. Though they have different visions about what the "right thing" is, Peter realizes that he and his friend actually share this passion—it's why they argue so much!

The next time they talk about politics, Peter is prepared. He leaves behind his judgments, biases and assumptions about what Mike believes. Instead, he *asks* him. Really asks. Mike is flattered by the attention and speaks more openly than he ever has before. He feels respected and actually listened to for the first time. Peter is pleased, and decides to take further action—would Mike be prepared to hear his side of things, too? Maybe he would be interested in reading some of Peter's favorite books on the topic?

This story has all the elements of empathy working together: open-mindedness, stepping into another's shoes and real, deliberate action.

Fast-forward a few months. Peter and Mike still disagree as much as ever. Neither has converted the other to their point of view, and nobody has "won." But in a sense, they have achieved something more worthwhile: their friendship is stronger than ever, their connection more honest and open, and they truly **see** one another. This is the perfect example of how emotional validation supersedes agreement and harmony. When both people willingly see and accept the other, what does it matter that they disagree on the details?

Takeaways

- Empathy and validation are two very closely linked concepts. Validation is when we convey our acceptance of another person's experiences and emotions, whereas empathy is when we see the world as they do and truly put ourselves in their shoes. One can validate without actually being empathetic and vice versa. However, when we combine the two, we get a powerful combination that can instantly uplift someone's mood by making them feel seen and heard.

- Cultivating empathy in ourselves is something all of us should endeavor to do. There are three main steps to do this. First, we must be open-minded. Second, we must learn to walk in other people's shoes. Third, we must communicate our acceptance of their experience in an appropriate manner.

- Being open-minded is a commonly exalted virtue that many of us can struggle with. We tend to have difficulties understanding the ways different people perceive the world and express emotions when these conflict with our own views. The best way to remedy this is to simply talk to people from different backgrounds and viewpoints. Expose yourself to different discourses and ways of understanding things. Travel far and wide if you can, and familiarize yourself with cultures where things are done differently from your own.

- Walking in someone else's shoes requires that we pay as close attention to them as possible so that we can understand where they're coming from and what influences are at play. We must suspend our own views and see the way from the other's lens. A great way to inculcate this skill is to simply read fiction. This puts you into the mind of a character that is not you, and you get to observe how they describe events, emotions, thoughts, etc.

- Lastly, our understanding is only worth something when we can communicate it well. Be careful in the verbal and non-verbal cues you send out. Respect boundaries when they're asserted and try to remember the things that are shared with you.

Chapter 6. Empathetic Communication

To continue in the spirit of practical, communicated acceptance, we will devote our final chapter to a more in-depth look at how we can show validation through empathy, both in how we express ourselves, and how we listen to the expression of others. Again, we are going a little further than validation here; it's wonderful to convey the message "your perspective is valid," but so much more powerful to say "your perspective is valid, and I have genuine understanding and compassion for it."

Empathy is something we feel for someone else. Empathic communication is expressing this empathy, and it's all about making sure the *other person feels that empathy*, too. In other words, the benefit of our empathy is to enrich the experience of someone else, and not just ourselves.

Empathetic Communication

Let's look at the basics of what makes any communication empathetic, bearing in mind the three important elements of empathy already outlined in the previous chapter. Here, we're going to look at all the ideas we've already covered in this book, but in a more practical way—what are the actual words we can use?

Before we dive into that, however, we need to consider a few important principles about communication in general. Firstly, we need to have a clear, proper understanding of what communication is. People are individuals, but they all exist in context to other individuals, to groups, families, and communities. We are all discrete beings, but

Making space, reflecting or reacting. Each has its place. You may find that all of these approaches are useful as you listen; you could start by making space and simply allowing people to speak, but gradually move on to more reflection and eventually display your own reaction.

Empathetic listening checklist

Have I been nonjudgmental?

Have I heard both the feelings and the facts?

Have I listened carefully—and demonstrated this?

Have I found a way to reflect, respond, ask questions or otherwise engage with what I've heard?

In the broadest sense, what does the speaker really want from me and how I can show this?

What has been the effect of my listening and how best can I adjust my approach?

The above checklist is something you can run internally during the conversation itself. If you begin with making plenty of space and find that the other person is very uncomfortable with too much silence and keeps seeking your feedback, then you can move more into reacting and reflecting. You can ask more questions or try to gauge what they would find most validating in the moment.

Just as you would with empathetic communication, **think about listening from the other person's perspective**. Why are they speaking? What do they want and need from the conversation and from you? Are they seeking reassurance or validation? Or do they just need to talk out loud and put their thoughts together? The only way you'll know is to listen, and watch the effect your listening has.

If you're ever in doubt about what to do with someone's emotion (for example, if they're angry or it's difficult to gauge their goal in sharing their experience), then it's always a good idea to ask questions. Whenever you ask a question, you are confirming that you are present and paying close attention, even if you might not yet understand perfectly.

Of course, this doesn't have to be a mysterious and underhanded process. You can also ask the person directly, depending on the relationship you have with them:

"How would you like me to support you right now?"

"It seems like you just need someone to listen, is that right?"

"Would you like to talk some more about XYZ or should we drop the topic?"

You can also talk directly about the conversation you're having, either during or after, and squeeze in some final validation before you end the talk:

"Thank you for trusting me enough to share that with me."

"I'm so glad we talked. I hope you know I'm always available if you need to discuss anything else."

"I appreciate that you offered that feedback."

"I think I can now understand your situation a lot better. You've explained yourself very clearly."

The approaches outlined above are just as useful in conflict or disagreement. In fact, complete attention and devoted listening is often *more* important when the other person is angry and hostile, since you cannot usually have a fruitful discussion with someone until they feel they've said their piece and been heard. If you offer up a feeble fake apology and immediately launch into excuses or justifications, you can expect the conflict to last far longer!

Empathetic communication and active listening are both skills that need to be practiced—understanding the theories behind them is only the first step. It's easy enough to agree that something sounds like a good idea in the abstract, but completely forget about it when you're in the heat of the moment. But persist in practicing these techniques during every real-life conversation you engage in, and you *will* improve.

As your ability for self-validation and self-compassion increases, so will your ability to really see and appreciate people, exactly as they are, with understanding and empathy. One final trick that almost seems too easy, is to simply announce your intention to be a better listener and a more empathetic communicator. You may be surprised at how well people respond when you genuinely open up to them and say, "I want to really see and appreciate this situation from *your* perspective. I'm trying hard to be a better listener. Will you help me understand?"

Takeaways

- The key to validating someone effectively is being able to communicate empathetically. But what is communication, really? Essentially it is the passing of a message between a sender and a recipient. The message must be framed in a way that is understandable to the recipient. One of the key elements of communicating successfully is that the speaker must have empathy. Thus, to ensure that your words are communicated effectively, you must be empathetic, which means you must make an effort to understand the recipient and the best ways to cater your message to them.

- Just like we have empathetic communication, there's also empathetic listening. Empathetic listening is very similar to active listening, wherein all of your focus is devoted solely to the speaker. There are a few different types of empathetic listening, such as making space, reflecting, and reacting.

- When you make space, you suspend your own ego and "make space" for the message that is being delivered through verbal and non-verbal cues. Things like making eye contact and having a receptive body language are all examples of making space.

- When we reflect, we're mirroring what someone has told us right back at them. This is the best and easiest way to make someone feel heard and understood because it gives them proof that you've been listening throughout. Try to keep your own insights out of the equation when reflecting and simply focus on projecting the same emotions and words that are being expressed to you.

- Reacting is the most common form of listening, but it's also the one where we should exercise the most caution. Reactions need not be comprehensive or something major. They can be subtle, like when we nod our heads along with the speaker. Like with reflecting, our reactions shouldn't be about our own viewpoints, but rather indications that we've understood those of the other person.

Summary Guide

CHAPTER 1. VALIDATION AS A COMMUNICATION SKILL

- When we validate someone, we convey our acceptance of that person's experiences, emotions, thoughts, and realities. Conversely, when we invalidate someone, we deny or minimize the importance of their issues and needs. Though validation is a common word these days, it's not always clear how best to or even why we should engage in it. The fact is that every person's experience is inherently valid and instead of exercising judgement, we should try and accept people as they are. However, acceptance must not be confused with agreement.

- The concept of validation is especially relevant in our present age because of how socially isolated we are as individuals. Validating someone is a way of expressing solidarity with them, and makes the other person feel heard and understood. It adds a richness and sense of ease to life that would otherwise be missing if we felt that we have to go through life's travails alone and without anyone else's support.

- Many people tend to confuse sympathy, empathy, and validation, and there is indeed significant overlap between the three concepts. However, sympathy is when we see other's experiences through our own lens and react accordingly. When empathizing, we try to relate to other's experiences the way they are experiencing them. Lastly, validation is merely expressing your belief that someone else's experience is inherently valid.

- It's natural to wonder to what extent and how often we should validate others. We can't always validate things, especially when doing so could have adverse effects. For example, validating someone's aggressive and potentially dangerous behavior is a bad idea. Similarly, we must be wary of energy vampire who suck the life out of you by endlessly complaining without taking any concrete steps to ameliorate their situation. Lastly, giving unsolicited advice is generally unadvisable, but if someone is actively looking for guidance from you, substituting it with validation isn't a good idea because it isn't serving any purpose.

CHAPTER 2. VALIDATION — THE BASIC STEPS

- Marsha Linehan has come up with a comprehensive, six-step model of validation that we can use when listening to others. Each step in this model relies on the previous one. One can't jump from step 1 to step 6; they must follow each step in the same order to validate someone in the best, most reassuring way possible.

- The first step in this model is simply being present. Here, you must actively listen to the other person and pay close attention. Give the other person subtle feedback through verbal and non-verbal cues which indicate that you're listening to them. This will make the other person feel more comfortable with you. The second step is called accurate reflection, and here you need to summarize what you've been told to provide further reassurance that you've understood what they've told you. Keep it simple, but significant.

- Next, try to read subtle cues the other person is giving. This involves some guesswork, but you only need enough information to be able to label their words with an emotion. For step four, try to contextualize the person's thoughts and emotions with either recent events from their life or past experiences which might be influencing their reaction.

- Step five is to simply reassure the other person that their reaction is reasonable and anyone else in their position would feel the same way. Lastly, for step six, you can relate their experiences with your own if you've been in a similar situation. Being vulnerable here can establish a stronger bond and invite further conversation and trust.

CHAPTER 3. INVALIDATION AND SELF-VALIDATION

- Invalidation is doing or saying anything that makes another person feel that their thoughts, emotions, or even their entire sense of self are

173

wrong and unreasonable. People who have been regularly invalidated during childhood develop severe mental and emotional issues in their adult life. They are at risk of developing mental health disorders, practicing invalidating behaviors themselves, having a weak sense of self, constantly doubting themselves, and so on.

- People who invalidate others generally do so for two reasons. First, they intend well but simply don't know the best way to validate someone else. So, they end up engaging in either minimizing, judging, or denying the other's issues. However, there is also another group of people who intentionally invalidate others, such as in the form of gaslighting. Here, people train others to doubt their own sense of perception about things by continuously invalidating them.

- Some of the most common ways in which we might invalidate others include using undermining language, having judgmental attitudes, trying to fix another person's problems when they just want to be heard, etc. Avoid using words like "but" by replacing them with "and" while also being mindful of your tone while conversing. Don't exercise judgement and remember that you are not being asked for a solution, the other person simply wants their thoughts to be heard.

- When someone invalidates you, it's essential to establish clear boundaries, especially if the other person is close to you. If not, you may simply choose to end the conversation and cease contact. But if they are close, you'll want to calmly use "I" statements to convey how the invalidation made you feel and set boundaries that establish how you want to be treated in the future.

- When another person doesn't give you the validation you wanted, practice self-validation. Use affirmations, journaling, practice positive self-talk, or you can even use Linehan's six-step model by yourself. All of these practices help you become self-sufficient and less dependent on others to affirm your thoughts and emotions.

CHAPTER 4. VALIDATION AND CONFLICTS

- It's one thing to validate someone when their grievances are aimed at someone else. It's another thing entirely to do so when you are the source of their frustrations. Another challenging scenario is validating someone when they're espousing views or thoughts that are morally abhorrent to you. However, in both these cases, it is essential that we focus on the person and not the content of their argument. Always remember that validation is not agreement; you can validate without accepting someone's views.

176

- There are three easy steps you can follow when trying to validate someone voicing objectionable statements. First, try to understand their emotions and viewpoint before attempting to get your own point across. Second, focus on the person, what they're going through and where they're coming from before judging. Third, focus and try to find commonalities between you two. Even when it seems like there aren't any, there likely are. You just need to avoid being so turned off by the conversation that you stop looking.

- It's easy to feel like you're doing something wrong by validating someone who says things you find disturbing or even horrifying, but it's important to keep in mind that validating does not mean agreeing. It's essential that we acknowledge everyone has an inner emotional reality that is valid in its own way and we have no right to judge them for it, especially when we haven't taken the time and effort to understand them properly.

- Validating someone who is mad at you is a subtle but highly useful skill. The main way to do this is to keep reminding yourself that the point is not to win any arguments and not to establish your superiority over the other. You are merely allowing the person to express and have their emotions accepted even if you don't agree with them. Listen to them attentively, accept responsibility for your actions, offer your side of things calmly and without invalidating what's been said, and end the conversation with further validation and framing the issue as a "we" problem rather than a "me vs. you" one.

CHAPTER 5. EMPATHY: BEYOND VALIDATION

- Empathy and validation are two very closely linked concepts. Validation is

178

when we convey our acceptance of another person's experiences and emotions, whereas empathy is when we see the world as they do and truly put ourselves in their shoes. One can validate without actually being empathetic and vice versa. However, when we combine the two, we get a powerful combination that can instantly uplift someone's mood by making them feel seen and heard.

- Cultivating empathy in ourselves is something all of us should endeavor to do. There are three main steps to do this. First, we must be open-minded. Second, we must learn to walk in other people's shoes. Third, we must communicate our acceptance of their experience in an appropriate manner.

- Being open-minded is a commonly exalted virtue that many of us can struggle with. We tend to have difficulties understanding the ways different people perceive the world and express emotions when these conflict with our own views. The best way to remedy this is to simply talk to people from different backgrounds and viewpoints. Expose yourself to different discourses and ways of understanding things. Travel far and wide if you can, and familiarize yourself with cultures where things are done differently from your own.

- Walking in someone else's shoes requires that we pay as close attention to them as possible so that we can understand where they're coming from and what influences are at play. We must suspend our own views and see the way from the other's lens. A great way to inculcate this skill is to simply read fiction. This puts you into the mind of a character that is not you, and you get to observe how they describe events, emotions, thoughts, etc.

- Lastly, our understanding is only worth something when we can communicate it well. Be careful in the verbal and non-verbal cues you send we are necessarily connected. What connects us? Communication.

When we communicate, three essential parts are involved: the one sending the message, the one receiving the message, and the message itself. The one sending the message encodes it in a mixture of verbal and non-verbal language. This message is communicated in some form, like in writing or in speech to the recipient, who must "decode" or understand what our message is. Validation is a kind of communication, which conveys the message of acceptance. Though we don't have enough space to dwell on the topic of communication too closely here, it's enough to say that the effectiveness of any communication comes down to how well the speaker conveys the message to the listener.

The success of communication relies on the empathy of the speaker, the openness of the listener, and the accuracy and appropriateness of the message. This is worth repeating: communication fails if the speaker lacks empathy, the listener doesn't want to listen, or the message is not sent in a language the listener even understands.

When we communicate, we have to imagine the person we are talking to. We have to picture who they are, what they're thinking, what they want, what they can understand, and the barriers to their hearing us. Can you see how empathy is not just a good idea for communication, but something fundamental to it? If we are just talking in a void, with no consideration for the ears that are hearing us, we are not communicating—we are just indulging in a monologue.

Another fundamental principle is that communication is not just words. As we've seen, there are many ways to convey the same message, and a lot can be "said" with facial expressions, posture, voice, even things like clothing or gestures.

Empathic communication, then, requires us to think carefully about who we are when we communicate, who we are talking to, and how we are framing our message. We know that if we're talking to a five-year-old, we explain ourselves differently than if we were talking to a fifty-year-old. We know that if we want others to accept our message, we sometimes need to soften it, massage it a little, reframe it to suit what we know are their tastes. And we also know that if we share in a completely different "language" to the person we're addressing, we may need to change ourselves and our expression if we hope to be understood.

This is the root of empathic communication: **We first understand the perspective of who we're talking to, and then we adjust the way we talk accordingly.**

Consider your own role in the communication process:

What is your communication style and how does this affect others? Is it appropriate in this context?

When it comes to communicating, what are you good at and what are your weaknesses, biases or blind spots?

If communication is already difficult, what barriers are you contributing to or maintaining?

Is the problem really about you and your message, or is it that you haven't yet practiced listening to the other side?

What medium are you using to communicate, what language are you using, what is your tone of voice?

Finally, what are you most trying to achieve in communicating? What do you hope to get from speaking out? Are you driven by ego, the desire to help, or are you succumbing to outside pressure? Consciously or unconsciously, what are your emotional motives for talking?

If you frequently feel misunderstood, it might be a question not of the unwillingness or inability of the other person to hear you, but of your message or the way that you are personally framing it.

Once you have a proper understanding of your role in the picture, you can look at the other person's. Here, you cannot make assumptions. You cannot guess that they know the things you know, care about what you care about, or share the same goals or even reference points for communication in the first place. Ask yourself:

Who are they? What do they value and why?

What is their communication style and how might this interact with yours?

What about them might prevent them from truly hearing you? How can you frame things in their "language"?

Put yourself in their shoes and imagine what they think of the message you're sharing.

What do they want; what is driving them?

What is their history and context, and how does it differ from yours? What are they familiar and unfamiliar with?

What assumptions and expectations of you might they hold?

Looking at both points of view, you can start to see potential barriers to understanding, limitations or disagreements. And this leads you to consider the final part of the puzzle: the message itself and how it can be crafted for maximum effectiveness.

What is at the heart of what you're trying to say? Why are you saying it?

What is the best format for this message? Does the medium match the message?

How long and how detailed should this message be?

What tone would suit it best? Intense and direct? Gentle? Playful and irreverent? Confiding? Neutral and professional?

What kind of language will be most effective—jargon or slang? Logical or emotional? Direct or suggestive? Would it work best presented as a narrative, a debate, a defense, a neutral report?

Should it be written or spoken? Shared digitally? Can images or metaphors help?

What are the possibilities for misunderstanding and how could you avoid them?

So many people think that communication comes down to what you say. But as you can see, it's also about who is saying it, and who is hearing it.

out. Respect boundaries when they're asserted and try to remember the things that are shared with you.

CHAPTER 6. EMPATHETIC COMMUNICATION

- The key to validating someone effectively is being able to communicate empathetically. But what is communication, really? Essentially it is the passing of a message between a sender and a recipient. The message must be framed in a way that is understandable to the recipient. One of the key elements of communicating successfully is that the speaker must have empathy. Thus, to ensure that your words are communicated effectively, you must be empathetic, which means you must make an effort to understand the recipient and the best ways to cater your message to them.

- Just like we have empathetic communication, there's also empathetic listening. Empathetic listening is very similar to active listening, wherein all of your focus is devoted solely to the speaker. There are a few different types of empathetic listening, such as making space, reflecting, and reacting.

- When you make space, you suspend your own ego and "make space" for the message that is being delivered through verbal and non-verbal cues. Things like making eye contact and having a receptive body language are all examples of making space.

- When we reflect, we're mirroring what someone has told us right back at them. This is the best and easiest way to make someone feel heard and understood because it gives them proof that you've been listening throughout. Try to keep your own insights out of the equation when reflecting and simply focus on projecting the same emotions and words that are being expressed to you.

- Reacting is the most common form of listening, but it's also the one where we should exercise the most caution. Reactions need not be comprehensive or something major. They can be subtle, like when we nod our heads along with the speaker. Like with reflecting, our reactions shouldn't be about our own viewpoints, but rather indications that we've understood those of the other person.

9 781647 432423